Dieter Duhm

FUTURE
Without War

Theory of Global Healing

VERLAG MEIGA

About the book:
The war industry is an integral part of our society. If we truly want a future without war we shall need another civilisation, another way of inhabiting our planet. True peace is not a slogan, true peace is a new form of living. Peace will emerge from social structures which do not destroy basic human values like compassion, trust, mutual support and solidarity, but rather create and preserve them. A worldwide cooperative of people is needed to develop the new communities. Already some of these centres would suffice to bring about global healing. We are faced with a huge opportunity. The book is addressed to all those who are ready and able to co-create a worldwide cooperative for a future without war and are willing to support this initiative with all means available.

About the author:
Dieter Duhm, born in 1942 in Berlin, he was a leading thinker of the movement of 1968, studied art history and psychoanalysis, and obtained a PhD in sociology. Shaken by the scope of global violence, he withdrew in order to develop a working model for a future without war. He developed the "Plan of the Healing Biotopes", a global peace concept, and has been working to realise it for 25 years. This led to the establishment of the "Healing Biotope I Tamera" in Portugal. Today he is working there together with approx. 150 co-workers, establishing a world model for peace.

www.dieter-duhm.de

Impressum

ISBN: 978-3-927266-24-7
© 2007, Verlag Meiga
Translated from the German by Sten Linnander and Frieda Julie Radford
Original Title: Zukunft ohne Krieg.
Cover Photo © Birger Bumb
Layout and Cover Design: Jana Mohaupt
Print: Books on Demand (BoD) GmbH, Norderstedt, Germany

Contents

Do we wish that the youth of the world no longer goes to war?
Then we need higher goals for life, a life worth living with better
opportunities to put the energy of youth into meaningful action

Do we wish to end worldwide sexual violence?
Then we have to create real living conditions under which sexual joy
can be experienced without violence, without humiliation and with-
out unnecessary restrictions.

Do we want to end the abuse of children?
Then let us build up living conditions where nobody thinks of viewing
a child as a sexual object.

Do we want to free the world from despotism, betrayal and lies?
Then let us build up real conditions under which despotism, betrayal
and lies no longer give any kind of evolutionary advantage.

Preamble of the Publisher

To introduce this book I want to relate a personal experience:

Yesterday evening I met a few women for a talk. It was a warm spring evening, we sat outside, surrounded by lovely flowers in bloom. In the growing twilight Luz Maria from Colombia told us the story of her life. She was visiting Europe for the first time. She is a 50 year old *campesina*, a peasant, who can neither read nor write. At the age of sixteen she was almost killed. The machete missed her head by inches, but hit her left thumb almost severing it. Her husband and her eldest son were killed years ago. Since then Luz Marina has cared for herself and her six children all on her own. The *campesinos* are easy game for the armed groups, be they military, police, paramilitary, guerrillas or simply armed groups of bandits who are not bound by any moral authority nor subject to the rule of law. Only in the last few years over 150 people from her village were killed, some of them in a most gruesome way.

Luz Marina however cannot go away. Where to? The situation is just as bad elsewhere; at least there in her village she has a small piece of land where she can grow food to meet the basic needs of her family.

The fate of Luz Marina is the fate of millions, probably billions of human beings who live on our planet today. Where should they go?

Future without War has been written in response to such fates.
The book wants to save people. To do so it sets aside all the sweeping gestures and trendiness of today's world of short-lived effects and advertising spots. The reader is asked to study its theory, sentence by sentence, thought by thought. And by so doing it conveys the logic how to effectively help the world.
This book explains how the earth can be healed.

The author, himself confronted by violence early on in life, has left all conventional paths behind and has dedicated his life to the question of how a non-violent world can be created. He is, as many visionaries are, way ahead of his time. He has had to overcome many barriers in a life that has been beset with difficulties and hostility. In this book he leads us into the intellectual and spiritual space of a "Healing Biotope", the first of which was developed a few years ago in Southern Portugal.

Apart from some biographical sketches, the book is a collection of texts and talks which he wrote and gave while teaching at the Peace School of Tamera. Repetitions in the content were often unavoidable but even so they can prove useful by helping the reader to follow the train of thought from different angles.

In this book Dieter Duhm hands on to the next generation the basis of his political knowledge for a future without war. He sheds light on the countless possibilities available to us human beings, if only we are ready to open upto new intellectual and spiritual resources. The Earth, her human societies, her crisis areas and trouble spots, her creatures, her atmosphere, her waters and biotopes can be healed just as the body of a human being can be healed, as soon as we discover the necessary healing forces and put them into action.

On first sight, the aims of the book appear impossible. Nevertheless, it does reveal new courses of action which have not yet been considered or tried before. It sets out a global vision where individual thoughts come together rather like the pieces of a jigsaw puzzle and bit by bit the full picture gradually develops until it all can be clearly seen. It is at this point that we are able to unerringly follow the path towards a humane future.

What is being taught in this book is the knowledge of a new era. It teaches us to no longer separate theory from experience, spiritual and intellectual work here and everyday life there, the objective world "out there" and a subjective world "in us". Equally it teaches us not to separate between those who live in crisis areas and those who do not, i.e. ourselves, who have a roof over our head and full refrigerator. We are all part of one and the same family of life. We all suffer from the same illness. Our own healing, together with help for the world's poor, and protection for the natural world are all part of one and the same process which we must adhere to and reinforce by adopting life-changing decisions.

It appears to me that in a book that claims to present a concrete concept for a future without war, it is essential to introduce the author and shed some light on his background.

What kind of human being is behind such thinking? What was his path to development?

The author Dieter Duhm was born in Berlin in 1942 in the middle of World War II. He experienced violence first hand, in Berlin during the nights of bombing, on the refugee trail to Southern Germany and then afterwards in his new homeland by Lake Constance. He was a stranger and was seen as not belonging in the village. One day, barely six years old, a group of local boys grabbed him, tore his clothes off, tied him to a lamp post and smeared him with tar from head to toe. Again and again they banged his head against a stone kerb. He had done nothing, but to them he was "the stranger". They needed someone on whom to take out their own anger and their own homelessness. It was there that he received his first lesson on the nature of fascism.

He was about 14 years old when he first heard of the concentration camps. At first he refused to believe that it was true and his mind struggled against the idea telling himself that they must all be criminals and as they must be adults they would not find it so hard or suffer too much. Then he began to persistently ask questions of his parents and of people he knew. He must have troubled them quite a lot. His hopes of finding easy answers soon faded the more facts his research unearthed. There was no consolation in Auschwitz: it was a reality, a reality that could never be undone.

He clung to one last hope that the horrors *were* the reality and would perhaps never be repeated. But also this hope shattered. Years later he became one of the leaders of the leftist German '68-Student-Movement. Together with his comrades he fought against imperialism and the Vietnam War. He saw the photos of Vietnamese women with their breasts cut off. He saw the pictures of people burnt by napalm. He realised then that this was the reverse side of Western morality and culture.

Then he experienced the murder of a man whom his comrades believed to be an informer. This made him realise that an elementary fact of political life is that ideological beliefs are interchangeable as long as man's character structure remains the same.

In other words it will all remain the same as long as human beings grow up under the same old conditions, as long as they are exposed to the same sexual prohibitions during puberty and as long as they experienced the same fear of loss and jealousy during adulthood.

Why was it that the visions of an ideal human society could not be realised? Because the obstacle does not exist in outer conditions only, but is to be found primarily in the inner structures of human beings and in their ways of thinking. It is impossible to build a free society with people who have been formed and shaped in authoritarian circumstances. It is impossible to create a humane form of free love with people who have been repressed and who have condemned sexuality. It is impossible to establish a non-violent society if inner impulses of hatred and violence are simply suppressed and left unresolved. A revolution that has not taken place in the inner realm will never succeed in the outer world. This is one of the lessons of history.
(D. Duhm: The Sacred Matrix)

However, the leftist movement did not go along with these ideas.

Dieter Duhm did not re-integrate himself into bourgeois society. He declined various offers for professorships. In the face of global violence he was not able to put up with the daily routine.

He decided to retreat to a lonely farm house in Lower Bavaria and there to reflect on it all. The massacre of My Lai and the massacre of the Second World War... - where did this continuum of violence stem from? How was it possible for the Holocaust to happen? How could good family men turn over night into concentration camp executioners? Is it possible to end global violence once and for all?

His country retreat turned into an intellectual and spiritual workshop for a humane future. He occupied himself with many different sources of thinking and wisdom, with Nietzsche, Hegel and van Gogh, Rudolf Steiner, Jesus, Lao Tse, Wilhelm Reich, Prentice Mulford, Teilhard de Chardin. Slowly the individual fragments of knowledge began to fall together and show a new overall picture, a preliminary stage for his later holographic view. A new intellectual and spiritual pattern began to form itself based on the latest findings of biology, cybernetics, psychoanalysis and mathematics as well as art, history and theology. A vision emerged: yes, it was possible! Peace could prevail.

Out of the vision he formulated a political concept beginning where wars are an occurrence of daily life and are forever breaking out anew as in the relationships between human beings, between man and woman, between children and adults, individuals and society, nature and man. It is in these areas that a change has to take place, where a shift in practise has to be shown, not only intellectually, or in words, but also by concrete example.

He began to put his ideas into practise, created in 1978 the first "Social Experiment", suffered many setbacks, met resistance, slander and hostility from society at large. He started from scratch again ever deepening and correcting his concept. Long years passed without any visible sign of success. But he kept at it.

His belief in that inner life pattern which in later works he calls the Sacred Matrix still grows. Although he turned away long ago from Christianity and all other religions, a prayer for help and support started to grow inside of him that became forever louder. He does not know to whom he prayed – it was simply prayer all by itself.

He founded his belief on compassion, research and experience

9

rather than on traditional dogma. Above all of this was his belief in humanity, in its powerful insight and capacity for truth.

In 1995, after long years of preparation, he finally founded the Tamera centre in Portugal together with his partner in life, Sabine Lichtenfels; the physicist Charly Rainer Ehrenpreis and others. Today, in 2007, about 150 people are working there engaged in the development of a community model without lies, without violence and without degradation. As a case model they research and bring about the social, ecological and technological aspects that can be the basis of a future world society.

Today, after almost 30 years of work, the project has entered a phase of realisation corresponding to the original dream.

The present book is something like a political legacy for the next generation. May the young people of all countries adopt its thoughts and may they cooperate to create a future without war.

I myself wish to express to the author my deeply felt and sincere thanks for his having shown us the truth of this unerring love for life.

Monika Berghoff
Publisher
Verlag Meiga

Chapter 1

Introduction

The Basic Political Thought

Global injustices are occurring on earth and they have indescribable consequences for all those affected by them. In many regions on earth the sufferng is unimaginable. Burning, mutilation and torture are the order of the day. The general public just looks away because it cannot bear the sight. We cease to react when we hear what human beings are doing to each other in crisis areas, what they are doing to children, to whole nations, and also to animals. The gruesomeness is too awful to be let into our souls. One knows that this is happening on every continent, but one has stopped reacting to it, and it has become an abstract and formal entity. Who, indeed, can react to what has happened in the former Yugoslavia and what is happening in the Caucasus, in Iraq, in the Congo, in Colombia, in Indonesia, in Russian prisons or Tibetan work camps? Who is still able to react to the fate of children, who are daily the victims of highly organised child pornography? And who is still able to react to the fate of millions of young people in western countries, who have neither a home nor a job to go to? And who is still able to react to the wild inner pain that lovers feel who having once sworn faithfulness are then forced to leave each other?

If we are able to recognise the dimensions of suffering, we will also be able to assess the dimensions of the healing that is necessary. There are possibilities for salvation. They can be found outside our conventional thinking patterns and forms of discussion, but they are as real as the wireless internet or the Hubble telescope in space. Who would have thought 50 years ago that such things would become reality? Given a different focus, the intelligence capable of developing electronic weapon systems is equally capable of developing systems of non-violent co-habitation on earth.

The present globalisation of violence can be overcome through a globalisation of peace, when we open up new intellectual, mental and spiritual resources. The old code of violence, formed by a five thousand year-long history, has generated morphogenetic fields of fear and mistrust. A new code must be developed, one that generates morphogenetic fields of love and solidarity. This is the global task.

I have written this book for the students of the Mirja Peace School in Tamera and for all those who desire to create similar centres at other places on earth. The main part consists of the theory that is described in Chapter 5. If someone asks you the question: why do you believe so firmly in the healing of humanity and of the earth, then that is where you will find the answer.

When the great murdering began some thousands of years ago, human beings lost their home on earth. This triggered a chain reaction of unspeakable violence, which continues to this day and through which a collective "pain body" has spread on earth. This is a "pain body" of the cultures and the religions, of displaced peoples and of communities that have been torn apart. It is a "pain body" of women, of abandoned children and of animals – branded in their souls and bodies with unforgettable methods. We all have "our Vietnam within ourselves" said the former American Vietnam soldier and current Zen buddhist Claude AnShin Thomas. We have all experienced a history of terror that we are trying to avoid by denying it, both within ourselves and amongst those who are victims today. We have built a wall around our hearts, so that we no longer have to come in contact with the pain. Locked up within this wall is the entire history of a worldwide trauma. Locked up is the physical torture and the pain of separation in love. Locked up are all elementary human emotions that we had when we were children.

Today, humankind has lost its anchor. Not only do we live with globalisation of outer violence, but also with globalisation of human alienation and loss of roots. Wars are not only taking place militarily, but also in love. Millions of people carry within them-

selves the pains of abandonment and of failure in love relationships. In the hearts of abandoned and betrayed children, the potential for violence is born and unloaded into today's world. There can
be no peace on earth as long as there is war in love. In Germany, a
human being commits suicide every 30 minutes. They do not die
because of hunger or cold, they die because there is no place where
they really belong, because there is no love in their lives and no
future to aim for. It is above all the inner human issues that are the
reason for the downfall of the world.

Under these conditions, individual appeals are not enough. A new
life needs new containers and new structures for everyone. Even the
best of people break down under the power of prejudice, slander and
violence. We need new social structures that make it possible to have
lasting trust, full integration of the sexual forces, durable love relationships and permanent cooperation with the forces of nature. The
only point where we still agree with the Marxists is that it is societal
existence that determines our consciousness; it is the structures in
society that collectively prevent or make possible trust and love.
Global healing cannot be achieved through individual therapy and
insight, but through the concrete development of new life systems
that serve the healing of all those involved. When the first of these
new centres– we call them Healing Biotopes – have been developed
and when their structures function, then a field emerges for the new
global information of peace. The peace information that has been
compiled in the cosmic data base enters into an "excited state" and
can manifest at various places on earth.

Apart from and behind the global pain, a different story is
unfolding, a kind of "parallel universe": the story of the Sacred
Matrix as the healing pattern for a larger world that wants to be
born. We are experiencing the true birth pangs of a new era. In this
book I will describe the healing powers of the world and I will
include them – as a hologram of healing – in my theory, because I
have experienced them myself in many situations that I would oth-

erwise have hardly survived.

The singer Hannes Wader sang the words:

Not only atrocities happen, already for so long.
I have seen the love, already for so long,
the belief, the courage, the hope, the blazing heat,
And what is happening in the faces of children.
Already for so long.

For us, who dedicate our lives to global peace work, it is not a matter, of course, that we are spared from being the subject of massacres. For us, it is not simply a matter of course that we are neither hungry nor suffering from cold. We take the fact that we live in safety as a gift of grace and as a special duty. As long as we are not part of the victims, we will do everything possible in order that some day there will be no more victims. The present concept for worldwide healing has been developed out of compassion and as a result of being a witness. The author has seen what cruelty means and also experienced it himself. It is no longer possible to look the other way, so the question becomes: what is to be done now?

No Revenge

The ideas of a realistic future which is worth living also have a very personal side to them. They release us from old images of hostility and fear, because they provide a more powerful perspective. Tamera is cooperating with peace workers in Israel and Palestine. A young Palestinian friend was shot at by Israeli soldiers. He was hit by three bullets. He fell in a coma. My daughter Vera visited him together with Israeli and Palestinian friends. When he woke up from the coma, his first words were: "No revenge."

The principle of revenge no longer serves, there is now a different one. Those who are our enemies today may have been our friends before. Those who are our friends today may have been our enemies before. In a coma, deep down where we no longer have a language, we are fully awake, but at a different level.

Those who have harmed us have suffered in similar ways, and they could be our friends. We begin to understand that, whatever we do unto others through our thoughts or deeds, falls back on ourselves. And we see that there is a different possiblity in life. For we are a part of the whole.

But we should never argue morally, as long as we are sitting in our warm living room, while outside terrible things are occuring which everywhere give rise to thoughts of revenge. Revenge is a principle of high energy. There are situations where one can follow no other thought than this one, because it is stronger than all other thoughts. I have experienced the truth in the saying that "revenge is sweet." Whenever people or peoples, who have experienced great injustices, follow the impulse of revenge, they feel no fear and they are willing to do anything. It is absurd but true that for millenia the energy of revenge was the energy of liberation. What can we offer to the soul of humans if we want to deprive it of liberation through revenge? Is there truly something better? Here, there is no room for empty slogans.

We are dealing with a reorientation of human thinking. In science this is called a "paradigm shift". Here, we are dealing with a paradigm shift in the deepest area of all. No revenge! Above all not when we see what they do. So what else, if not revenge? Reconciliation? How can you be reconciled with someone you hate? If the word reconciliation is to have any meaning at all, we must invent something for our souls that truly releases us from revenge and opens us up for reconciliation. This cannot consist of moral or religious appeals. It must be much more, much deeper, much greater.

A Vision

Sun Bear, a native American tribe elder said once:
Sometimes I dream that I am at a place where small groups of peo-

ple are approaching over a hill. We all embrace each other and call out: "Brother, sister, you have survived!" All "isms" have disappeared. We no longer say: "Which religion do you belong to? To what do you belong? None of this is of importance anymore.

I see a new generation of pilgrims from all countries travelling across the earth. They are not bound to any nation, language, race, culture or religion, to riches or possessions. They help in areas of crisis, they visit holy sites and they are on the way to centres, to new anchorages. They encounter each other at campfires, in barns or hostels, share their bread and develop a new quality of community, hospitality and willingness to help. In this way a young world citizenship of a new kind and beyond all institutions will come into existence – a different type of globalisation will take place. This development is supported by the emergence of completely new centres spreading slowly across the earth. We call them "Healing Biotopes" or "Peace Villages". They serve the pilgrims both as hostels and as places to study and work in. In these centres concrete research is conducted, facilitating the development of a technological, spiritual and social basis for a non-violent world society. The centres stay in touch with each other through the growing flow of pilgrims. They are aware of each other, they are on the same path, and they have taken on responsibility for the future of the planet. The beginning of a new culture, the dawn of a new era.

May the youth of all countries step out of their pasts and enter into the possibility of a new era of planetary thinking, planetary friendship and planetary joy. May the young people from Toronto, Sydney or Nairobi, from San Francisco or Kiev come together and meet. May they celebrate their new world community in Colombia or with the Zapatistas in Mexico, in Bethlehem or in Tamera. May they draw and actualise the information and forces from the world code that will lead us into a future worth living on a wonderful planet. They will do it, the "Movement for a free Earth" is under way!

A Note about Sexuality

In this book we keep touching on the sexual issue. We assign it a higher position and importance than is normally the case in the philosophical or spiritual discussions of our time. In order to recognize its healing function, we need an intellectual foundation outside of all religious and moral thinking. This is an intellectual foundation that engrains itself in our bodies, just as the old systems of blame and fear have done. In short, we need a new spiritual body culture. We have a long way to go before we are there. Through literature I am aware of three people who have discovered the path of a coming transformation in the bodily area – without, however, recognizing the importance of sexuality in this. These three are Sri Aurobindo, the "Mother" of Auroville, and the brilliant Satprem, who has formulated both their ideas in a fascinating language and has developed them further. We can find one highlight of his explanation of this new path of a spiritual body culture in his book "On the Way to Supermanhood" in the chapter "Victory over Death". Reading it, one gets a vivid feeling for the great transformation that we - together with the whole earth - are facing today.

The path of a new body consciousness must integrate sexuality, for it contains a key for a new connection between body and soul. If it is integrated intellectually and spiritually, it ensures a deep balance that the human being has been seeking for millenia, that he has found and has lost again.

Eros is a world power that runs through everything. As an example, one can read the amazing book by Renate Daimler entitled in German "Verschwiegene Lust. Frauen über 60 erzählen von Liebe und Sexualität" ("Silent Desire. Women over 60 Speak of Love and Sexuality").

Here, we no longer need to lie or pretend to be innocent, ignorant or even indignant. The code of peace that we are seeking and realising is a code for the reunion of the sexes on the intellectual and sexual foundation of solidarity and partnership. Riane Eisler called it the code of "Gylanie". It lies beyond chauvinism, feminism and all other "isms". It does not exist within any religion, nor is it written in any charter. Up to now it only exists in the unrestrained longing of millions of men and women on planet earth. Millions of men and women have protected themselves from it and simply run away, creating religions and waging wars, because they did not know the code. Once we know it, including its intellectual foundation, the result is almost automatically a new overall view of human culture and civilisation on our planet. **There is a point in the relationship between the sexes, where the decision is made if there will be war or peace on earth.**

We need new interpersonal experiences in order to understand these connections fully. Tamera has been established in order to create the social and ethical foundation for this. This is not achieved through quick sex and uncommitted contacts as we have been accused of in some of the media. In truth it can only be achieved through a new form of human relationships within a new framework of human community and commitment. Liberating and healing sexual love is probably the deepest and most encompassing task facing the 21st century.

Chapter 2

The War Society and its Transformation

A manifesto, written March 2005

(This text is available as a file in various languages at: www.dieter-duhm.de. We appreciate any help in distributing it.)

The external trigger for the following text was the extremely cruel murder of Luis Eduardo Guerra, director of a peace village in Colombia, together with seven more inhabitants of the village, among them women and children. It is one of these daily details that accompany globalisation today. Now our friend Gloria Cuartas, who protected the Colombian city Apartadó for years as its mayor, is receiving death threats. We have been in contact with these people for several years now.

A war similar to the one in Colombia is taking place in many parts of the world today. The following text is therefore not about one particular country but about the situation of the whole earth.

The world-wide war is rooted in the deepest structures of our civilisation and therefore cannot be overcome through appeals for peace, enlightenment and resistance. Global peace work needs a new global concept for a future without war.

The US is preparing its next crusades within the context of their "New World Order". They are planning the "Greater Middle East" project, an enormous free trade zone all the way from Morocco to Pakistan. This is the context for the planned wars against Iran and other countries such as Syria etc.

In spite of all diplomatic declarations, it is clear that this war has been planned, just as the war in Iraq was planned long before the search for alleged weapons of mass destruction began.

The streets in the villages and cities in Iran, on which the children are playing today, could very well soon look like the streets of Falluja, the devastated city in Iraq.

Is it known what war means? Does one know the unbearable pain of people who suffocate beneath debris, who are crippled or burnt? This and nothing else is war. The economic, political and military power cartels know that children die, freeze and starve as a result of their policies of conquest – and yet they continue to follow them. They know that families are torn apart and communities are destroyed – and yet they do it. They talk about peace, freedom and democracy and kill all freedom fighters who stand in their way. They have constructed a world of consumerism that results in slavery, despair and collapse on the other side of the world. Behind the figures of the stock market, there is the suffering of innumerable people and animals. More people die from the consequences of colonisation and globalisation than ever died in a war. Can we continue to enjoy our privileges and limit our efforts to words? We need to find real ways to free the earth from war.

We indirectly contribute to the war because we do not have the time to understand what is really going on there. Our culture is arranged so that nobody has the time to understand what is really going on. We are a part of the war because we participate in a civilisation which generates war everywhere. War is a component of our civilisation, our economy, our consumerism and our ideas about life. Our own Western society lives from the armament and weapons trade, from war against nature, from war against villages and farmers in the "Third World", from war against love, from war against our mental/spiritual anchors and homelands of humankind. This war claims its victims in Afghanistan and Iraq, in Latin America and Palestine, but it also claims its victims where there is supposedly peace and democracy: in the offices and factories, in schools and families, in love relationships and ruined marriages, in the situation of homeless youth, in the sexual misery of the youth, in organised child abuse as uncovered lately in Belgium (Dutroux) and many other European countries. And finally in the hopeless situation of people who cannot handle the lies of the existing culture any longer and who can no longer cope with the mechanisms of existing conditions.

And are not the slaughterhouses, the fur farms and the animal laboratories a part of the daily war as well?

Is it really necessary for the progress of a culture to be linked to such an amount of suffering in the animal world?

There is a solution. We can recognise it if we look at the whole of contemporary life on earth from a great enough mental/spiritual distance.

See the earth as a living organism, whose organs are connected to each other through certain frequencies. You yourself are an organ of this organism. Through your thoughts, words and deeds you send out certain frequencies which serve either peace or war.

We can recognize that we are a part of the global war as long as we are controlled by thoughts of fear, anger or revenge. Consequently, let us create places where we find the strength to no longer resonate with the powers of war – neither those in the world nor those in ourselves.

We will recognise that victims and perpetrators often are connected through analogue structures and that you yourself could be a victim as well as a perpetrator. It is a deeply mutual, historically grown structure of suffering that creates the victim as well as the perpetrator. Also the perpetrators have been victims before, they too have been robbed of their trust, their love, their human home. They also come from living conditions that produce violence. Alice Miller researched and described the living conditions of well-known violators. As a child, the Serbian dictator Milosevic witnessed the suicide of both of his parents. Goethe's 'mignon question' can be asked of even the toughest killer: *What have they done to you, poor child?*

Try to understand... You will understand that this is not about sentimentality, but about a collective basic fact of our current civilisation. It is about the drama of the loss of roots, the drama of disastrous love relationships, the drama of homeless children and the drama of separation and human deprivation. These are no longer private problems. They constitute the social and human drama of our times. Behind the world-wide epidemic of relentless violence hides the experience of a pain that cannot be dealt with in any other way. And yet it can be healed.

That is the global core issue, which we have to work on. The question is: how do we end the constant reproduction of the pain of separation, the fear of loss and deprivation? Or more positively: how do we create real living and loving conditions which serve the growth of trust and solidarity among all beings? We do not only need a solution for the victims. We need a solution for the whole of humankind. And last but not least: we need a solution for the animal world.

Imagine that there were a few places on earth with a few hundred people each, from where a concentrated information of peace is input into the frequencies of the world with a high intensity. They would have peace between each other, peace between the genders, peace between adults and children, and peace with the beings of nature. The global cycle of violence would be radically broken in these places. What effect would this have on the whole? Whatever happens to a part of the whole can happen to the whole as well – because we are all connected through a consistent code of life (DNA), consistent basic information, and a consistent holographic structure. In other words, this means that a radical modification of our way of living together with each other and with nature would have a high probability – if it really happened in a few places – of affecting the whole in the sense of morphogenetic field-building. (These thoughts are elaborated in more detail in Chapter 5 and 6.)

Do not say too quickly: this is not realistic. In a multiple universe there are many possibilities of existence. Which one is realised depends on the decisions we make. Should not humankind, which has the intelligence to develop self-steering rockets, also be able to jointly muster the intelligence to realise a positive variation?

There is an "objective vision" of peace, which is anchored as a real possibility in the structure of reality. It is not subject to personal randomness. It is the original image of the holographic film of the universe, it is the entelechial core of all things, it results from the systems of resonance of the world, it is laid out in the genetic code of our cells, and it is embedded in our consciousness as an accessible possibility. We can call it the Sacred Matrix.

In former centuries the attempt was made to capture and express this Sacred Matrix in harmonic numbers, in geometric patterns, in proportions of temples and cathedrals. We, as modern people, have to transfer it to real living conditions, working conditions, technology and organisation, to social structures and ecological ethics. **Society needs a new operating system to realise the peace code. The existing culture is an operating system of dominance, fear and violence. The Sacred Matrix is an operating system of openness, transparency and connectedness. It is today's human task to create initial functioning centres and models for this new operating system. We call them Peace Villages or Healing Biotopes.**

If we are successful in creating new communities on a few places on earth which are coherent with the Sacred Matrix then, with high probability, this would result in a global field effect. This in turn would be able to free up those powers of peace and healing that today are veiled behind fear and worry. Please give yourself the time to recognise this process. (It is as if a holographic film would be exposed to a laser beam at a new angle: a new image shows up, reality changes.)

The path of overcoming the war does not end in enlightened inwardness. The world does not only need good people, most of all it needs new life forms for a future without war. It needs models for a new civilisation, so that we can start to settle our planet in a new manner which is coherent with the laws of life.

23

To realise peace, we have to know what peace is. We have to learn the rules of trust and love. We are approaching areas, which up to now have been attributed to religion or deep psychology. But is not this exactly the quality of a new way of thinking that includes the realisation that these "inner" realms of the human being have an eminent political meaning? If millions of people die every day of unfulfilled love, of hate and jealousy, is this not a political issue of the first order?

We learn the laws of universal peace by learning the laws of universal community. For all life exists in community. If we want to survive, we need new forms of community: community with people and peoples, with animals and plants, with all beings of nature and Creation. We need communities of co-evolution, of co-operation and mutual support for all participants, because they all follow the same urge of life. All are guided by the One Being, One Consciousness, the One genetic code. All together form the big family of life on earth.

The rediscovery of community, the ability to live communally, and the willingness to cooperate with all beings – these are key tasks of our time.

The well-known biologist Lynn Margulis said it like this:

If we wanted to survive the ecological and social crisis which we have caused, we would have to engage in radically new and dramatic community enterprises.

A German rock band ("Die Ärzte") sang:

Your violence is a silent scream for love. Your military boots long for tenderness.

Here, the connection between deprivation of love and readiness for violence is clearly illustrated. They continue:

You never learned to articulate yourself, your parents never had time for you … Because you have problems that nobody cares about, because you are afraid to cuddle, that is why you are a fascist.

These are connections that we have to see and change if we want to put an end to war.

The collective expansion of violence, which we are experiencing on earth, is the explosion of energies that have been blocked for a long time and that did not fit into the established system. The American or Russian or Israeli guys, who roam through Baghdad or Grozny or Ramallah in tanks and shoot to loud music, come from backgrounds in which they could not give these overflowing energies a positive direction.

Sabine Lichtenfels, the co-founder of Tamera, writes:

War comes from energies that have been held back for a long time. War comes from considering part of your soul as bad, judging it and thus withholding this part of your strength from the world, until it breaks out on its own and becomes destructive.

Under these circumstances we understand the sadistic cruelties that accompany every war, e.g. the sexual torture in Iraq. Whenever sexual energies cannot be integrated humanely, they break through violently. Whenever a healthy feeling of self-worth cannot arise because people live under wretched conditions, the feeling of self-worth is established through violence.

A young man was asked why he is a mercenary. He answered:

Because I want to become a real man.

He has to be harsh and learn to kill in order to be a real man!

We will not overcome these problems only by political resistance and moral appeals or by going within spiritually. We definitely need new ways of living together, new communities and new living spaces in which it is possible to become a real man by softer means, where one is not scared of love and one does not need military boots to hide one's own longing.

If we want to put an end to war, we need to end it where it is created and born each day anew: in our daily living conditions, in the constant stress of mindless and monotonous work, in the methods of profit maximization and distribution, in offices and factories, in schools and families, in the tragedies of love, in our ideas of being a man or being a woman, of sexuality and love, in the much too small cages of our professional, social and sensual lives.

Do we wish that the youth of the world no longer goes to war?
Then we need higher goals for life, a life worth living and better opportunities to put the power of the youth into meaningful action.

Do we wish to end world-wide sexual violence?
Then we have to create real living conditions under which sexual joy can be experienced without violence, without humiliation and without unnecessary restrictions.

Do we want to end the abuse of children?
Then let us create living conditions where nobody even has the thought of seeing a child as a sexual object.

Do we want to free the world from despotism, betrayal and lies?
Then let us establish real conditions under which despotism, betrayal and lies no longer have an evolutionary advantage.

Do we want people to find their anchor in the spiritual world?
Then let us create social structures that make this anchor possible.

Let us not only dream, talk, wish, and make appeals, but let us **build it up, really build it!**

The world will only turn to the better when we demonstrate that it is possible. For that we have to create convincing models. The know-how exists or is already well in hand and only waiting to be implemented in suitable locations. Social as well as technological concepts are ready to be implemented in future-oriented peace villages, but until now they could not be realised at the necessary scale due to a lack of financial and media support. If you have money, please support the development of such models. If you are a journalist, please help to spread this positive information. If you are well known, please use your name and influence to redistribute money.

We must do all this if we are serious about wanting to end the war in which our current world is engaged.

We thank "amnesty international" and all other peace groups for their efforts. We feel connected to the people who protect life in many places of the world and resist global injustice. But additionally we have to make the positive aim of humankind visible. Let us create the first convincing models and realise the existing concepts. We look forward to working with everybody who wants to co-operate with us in this sense.

The world needs the confederation of the most committed peace workers now, to create a new forum on earth: a world-wide co-operative for a future without war.

In the name of our children and all coming generations.
In the service of all Creation.

Chapter 3

The Totality of Possibilities

World matter knows no borders. It is open in all directions, it is multidimensional in itself and it is continually changing its outer manifestations. There is a totality, which is more total than everything else that we have been able to imagine so far, namely the totality of the possibilities contained in world matter. Fixed reality does not exist. There is no ultimate law of nature defining borders – the only borders that exist are those we have made ourselves. Therefore, a very determined will exists to move these borders or rather to dissolve them. This makes me think of adventurers, athletes and sportsmen such as Alexander von Humboldt, Rüdiger Nehberg, Klaus Hätzel, Reinhold Messner and Prentice Mulford. Part of the structure of the human will is a growing inner process of decision-making that all of a sudden solidifies into a final conclusion: Yes, it is possible! Yes, healing is possible! Yes, this body can become healthy again! Yes, this nightmare can be ended! Yes, this new earth and this new heaven, this totally new form of life, consciousness and society are all able to manifest themselves! Yes, reconciliation can take place even between Israel and Palestine. Or, as Ibraim Abuleish of Sekem, Egypt says: "Yes, we can turn the desert into a blossoming oasis!" Yes, we can turn this oppressed planet into one huge paradise!

A glance into nature shows us the possibilities of Creation in the Multiverse. The infinite richness of forms of both flora and fauna on the ground, beneath the water and in the air, gives us a foretaste of what is possible. The infinity of manifested forms are a portent of the possibilities that have not yet manifested but that exist in latent space and are waiting to be called forth from what David Bohm calls the "implicit order". A small twist of perception, a small change in the frequency of consciousness, a small deviation from the usual path will open up a new world – rather like the small twist of a kaleidoscope that creates a new and orderly pattern. Alongside the visible, manifest world, there seems to exist an infinite number of parallel worlds. At any moment one or the other can manifest itself depending on the angle with which the "beam of reference" enters.

Sai Baba manifests a dollar bill; Rolling Thunder creates a thunderstorm in Chicago; Jesus feeds the five thousand; the Jansenites withstand the stake and the muskets; incurable patients are healed on the spot; the Dutchman Mirin Dajo has a dagger pushed through his chest and pulls it out without being harmed. Miracle over miracle, all generated by a frequency change of consciousness, a "shift of the angle with which the beam of reference enters the holographic film" and an appropriate little "jump sideways" and we are in another reality. At the "Basel PSI Conference" Uri Geller demonstrated how seeds germinate in his hand.

We are entering a new age. We will notice that leaps of dimension are entirely natural and correspond to the rhythms of evolution. We will learn to bring them about consciously, provided that they are necessary for the humanisation of our planet. We will abandon the old beliefs and dogmas of illness, deprivation and decay. There are no ultimate laws about old age and death. We begin to become conscious embryos of ourselves and we begin to recognise how much we have impeded growth by putting a stop to it ourselves. Evidence from pre-historical times lets us suspect that in some ways we may have been here before. We begin to suspect that the universe is invested in the immeasurable structures of our body, from brain cells to the brain itself. Under such circumstance it seems strange that we keep looking backwards to what has been possible up to now when we look at what possibilities we have today with regards to peace work, the utilisation of solar power or the development of new social and economic structures. We refer to alleged laws of nature that have never existed in real terms. What seemed to us to be laws of nature were, in truth, but statistical laws describing the behaviour of man and matter – valid under the conditions of explicit societal circumstances and the structures of thought that went with them. They were historical laws and not eternal ones.

I would like to quote Prentice Mulford who, like no other, knew how to formulate such facts in a most impressive manner. Note that these sentences were written in the 19th century!

"It is no more due to the unavoidable course of nature that the human body decays …or that letters can be expedited only by the postman instead of by an electric spark.

It is the impertinence of dumb ignorance to want to make an assertion about what lies in the law of nature and what does not! It is a capital error to look back on the small piece of the past that is available to us and to take this to be the unmistakable sign for all that will ever happen from thereon until eternity. "
(Mulford, The Nonsense of Life and Death).

What is possible and what is not possible? Who is it that is asking this? Who is giving the answer? Who can determine the mental and spiritual framework and who controls the conditions that make both the questions and the answers possible? What do we know about ourselves and about the world that would allow us to talk about "laws" and "limits"?

Is not our own body a total, a super-total miracle? Every second, 10 to 100 billions of cells, each with a built-in minicomputer, accomplish a perfectly coordinated output, producing peak performances such as playing the violin, executing mechanically precise motions or circus acrobatics! Who has masterminded all this? Who has constructed the cells? Who had the intelligence to coordinate them in such a way? Has anyone seen the master builder?

When I see myself in the mirror and get scared of becoming too fat, a billion cells will immediately be mobilised in order to actualise the image of getting fat. Synchronous with this image or with the thought, all bodily functions which serve its realisation become operational and are triggered into action, regardless of whether we are dealing with a desirable image or an apprehensive thought. The deciding factor is the concretisation of the image that is connected with the thought. It is always the visualised image that is inherent in our thought. If millions of cells react instantaneously to such an image of thought with the single aim of realising it – then what if all of humankind did it? What if millions or billions of people are swept up by one image of thought and react in the same way? Is this not an almost unimaginable possibility for either evil or good? Did not the terrible times of the Crusades, the Inquisition or fascism provide enough proof of these possibilities? Would it not now be timely to use the same context for new and better aims, better images of thought?

The heaven and the earths that have been in existence so far have all been created based on an array of natural laws being formed under certain evolutionary conditions and through the development of human consciousness. It was a historical and for the most part horrible era that generated the seeming laws, limits and definitions, the many probabilities, possibilities and even more impossibilities.

The "Great Possible" appears to the extent that it becomes possible for us to segregate the world and to free it of its definitions, judgements and commentaries, which after all are our own and not those of the world. The limitations that we place upon the world seem to exist exclusively in our head. Therefore something has to happen within ourselves if we want to touch, enter and experience the "Great Possible". Whatever may happen within our selves on this path, whatever the seekers will find in terms of methods and experiments, it will always end with the same One. We will experience the "Great Possible" when we have stopped reacting to the world with fear. When we create structures in which the age-old fear disappears, trust arises - trust amongst one another, trust in nature, and trust in the sacred laws of life.

After all that we know about the construction of the world today at the end of the materialistic era, we must assume that the intrinsic basic matter of the world does not consist of material substance but is rather a substance made of ideas, visions, concepts and information! Knowing this represents the most central mental and spiritual paradigm shift of our times. It will radically change natural science and technology as well as our own daily habits. We stand at the beginning of a revolution, and it will sweep right across us, if, right from the start, we try to lock it into a cage of thought that is too confined, as Einstein said: "Nothing we are able to think is impossible." A future human civilisation will either be fundamentally different from the present one or else it will no longer exist.

I thank all those pioneers who by the power of thought, by the force of their intellectual and visionary endeavours are have prepared a new civilisation. I particularly thank all those who are currently doing so. We must communicate with each other!

Chapter 4

The Realistic Expectation of Salvation

I want to begin with moving words by Teilhard de Chardin, which he wrote in the face of worldwide misery:

My God, as well as my human dignity, forbids me to close my eyes to it like an animal or a child would do - that I do not succumb to the temptation to curse the universe and the One who created it - help me to worship it by seeing You concealed within.

The great liberating word "Lord" is the word that reveals and takes effect at the same time. Say it once more to me, Lord: "Hoc est corpus meum." (This is my body).

Truly, this sinister and dark something, the ghost, the storm – if we want it, you are it! "Ego sum, nolite timere." (It is I, do not fear).

"This is my body." This is All, the Whole. IT is always present. IT is neither the old God, nor the God of the old religions, nor the new God of some new religion. IT is the genius of the world, which consists of the coherent vibrancy of all things, all molecules and galaxies. This God is not external or above the world, rather, he (or she) is immanent resonance. Where things vibrate together, large forces are generated and large creations emerge. When the world vibrates coherently, healing occurs. It seems as if an inner world operator is aligned to create healing and to repair the Whole wherever it is damaged. Any damage is followed by feedback, i.e. this or that has to be done for you to remain whole and sound. It appears to be a cybernetic automatic control, which exists within all organisms. They are all aligned with healing, health, harmony and functioning interplay – otherwise this world machinery could not function.

We can probably only understand the Whole when we begin to understand our own simple everyday life. As an example, I am standing in the kitchen peeling vegetables and cut my finger. Immediately the forces of healing become active within the cells of my finger. The next day the wound is healed. Why? Who does this? I myself have not done it. What kind of miracle force is at work here and produces the healing?

Another example: man opens up a quarry in a landscape and nature is wounded. After some years the quarry is shut down. After a while the wound will be covered by the first plants that are needed for the healing. A real healing biotope emerges. We can observe this through small things, such as when we dig a trench on our property to install some pipes. After the work has been done, we cover it with earth and watch what happens. After a while we see how certain plants grow – healing plants – which heal the wound and create the basis for healthy growth. It is interesting to note that these healing plants are at the same time medicinal plants for the human being (stinging nettle, ribwort, etc.). In a word, nature is an organism that rebuilds and regenerates itself by means of its own healing power.

I ask that these simple examples be taken seriously – they count as evidence. Why should it be different with the human being? We are part of nature, we are her seeing eye, her organ of thought. What happens within my finger or in the quarry is a small symbol of the energy cycle of universal life. Once we begin to see and understand this, it will free us from all artificial therapies. "It" - that is life itself. It is life itself that has the power to heal. It is the universal overall information of the World Whole which at any moment and at any given place in the world can effect healing, provided that we are awake enough to receive it. This overall information is inherent in all the information carriers of our living world – from the information chains of the DNA to the synapses of the brain. The reality of the Sacred Matrix is always there; the healing information is ever present. The world is sound, in its innermost core it cannot not be sound. Otherwise it could not exist, and the same is true of us. Even in the worst of souls there is an intact core. This is what Teilhard de Chardin expresses in his prayer: "Hoc est corpus meum." And even if we do hear and experience so many cruel things, let us establish places where we no longer have to believe in infinite barbarianism because we recognise and realign with the spirit of the Whole.

Many people believe that war is part of life. They quote Heraclitus, the father of antique philosophy in Greece, with his famous words: "War is the father of all things." I do not know what he truly meant by these words. All I know is that war is the father of all things only as long as the mother of love is excluded. It is not very intelligent to believe that what has been going on for so long must stay that way. This much is true: war has dominated the thinking of mankind for thousands of years. The structures of suffering remain the same as long as the same train of thoughts, the same DNA information is called forth and the same synapses are activated in the brain. War is then part of life, to the same degree as jealousy is part of love. Do we seriously want to remain victims of such a fatal view? Did not evolution lead our technical world right up to the wireless internet and show that totally new possibilities exist? If we start today to create new connections, activate new information, follow new paths and switch on new synapses, if we develop new living situations and places where we can begin to do this continually and concretely, then a new world will emerge, as certainly as the old one did. The fact that the old world came into being is almost proof enough that a new one can be generated.

Through thinking, meditating and praying, through music and dance, through suitable nutrition and physical training we are capable of refocussing our antennas and strengthening our healing frequencies. There are no possibilities that are closed to us. Healing can occur even in the darkest of cellars, as was shown by the French resistance fighter Lusseyran, who survived the concentration camp of Buchenwald. If our senses are directed towards the presence of the Sacred Matrix, it will be effective at every place on earth. All the information that is necessary for the healing of humanity and the earth already exists and can be recalled if we prepare adequate base stations. These base stations consist of the human organism and the human community.

In our communities, we notice how slowly and gently, but also reliably and deeply, a new bio-energetic and bio-genetic path unfolds. This occurs when human beings get together to seriously end the world of war by being truthful amongst themselves and by generating a new hologram of trust. In this hologram of trust, lovers feel safe in their firm knowledge that they will never be betrayed again and children no longer need to be afraid of adults. Here, animals can approach human beings without having to be afraid of their barbarism and healing occurs between ourselves and all fellow creatures. Then we can say what Ruth Pfau has said: "Our last word will be love."

Ruth Pfau, the untiring woman doctor who cares for leprosy patients in Pakistan, Patch Adams, the doctor whose appearances as a clown make children who have been burnt by fire bombs in Afghanistan laugh again and Rüdiger Nehberg, with his commitment to end circumcision in Ethiopia - I thank such friends all over the world. All that has been done up to now by individual pioneers will now be integrated through the concrete development of healing centres. We are entering a new world. For ourselves and for subsequent generations, we will fully regain the brief experience that is shared by all those who have ever fallen in love: The bliss of eternal life, the joy of being here on earth, as well as in the "afterlife". We will live to see that there is no longer a difference between the two, since there is only the one life, which is sound and undamaged. "Our last word will be love."

Chapter 5

Theory of Global Healing

(The following chapter contains a new version of the Political Theory, which provides the basis for a possibility for unusual political and global action. The theory already exists in its previous versions published in the books "Political Texts for a non-violent earth" and "The Sacred Matrix". The versions differ in terms of didactics and the choice of words, but not in terms of content. They assume that there is a unity of the world, that all beings are engaged in encompassing basic communication and that there is a principle of field creation in holistic systems. Publisher's note.)

The cosmic world that has brought us forth and the societal world that we ourselves have created have drifted apart too far. Universal principles of life collide with the habits of a profit-oriented society. The human society inhabiting our planet is integrated in the cosmic order of a universe that to us is still largely unknown. It is in this order that we breathe and pulsate. Global healing emerges by consciously reuniting with the higher orders of the bio-cosmos. Human relationships, human love, human work and human community must reconnect with the comprehensive body of the larger whole.

The old notions of religion and politics have become redundant. We need a new solution for human life on our planet. No longer can we limit ourselves to treating the afflicted areas individually, since there would be no end to it. We need a solution for the whole of the planet, a basic healing for human beings and the earth, a fundamental new orientation for our cohabitation with all fellow creatures. - These were the basic thoughts with which the Project of the Healing Biotopes began 20 years ago.

Part 1: An Outline of the Theory

(Lecture without notes at the Summer University 2006 in Tamera)

The basis for the theory that is presented here is a world view that we can call "holographic cosmology". We all come from the universe, not only from Earth. We therefore all have within us the same latent cosmic knowledge, a store of memories and cosmic consciousness, which is at our disposal, and which we can use at any time, as long as we know how to use it. We call this storehouse the "cosmic database". What knowledge we base our lives, our actions and decisions on depends on what information we "download" from the cosmic database.

The knowledge that I am speaking about is always latently present. The miracle that we are waiting for can occur here and now, if we enter into the correct connection to the cosmic database. The cosmic database is constantly present, here, at this moment, just as radio waves, which nobody sees or hears, are present and surround us all the time. All we need to do is turn on a radio to hear the inaudible. The parts of reality that we can receive depend on our receivers. We experience the same "miracle" with TV or the internet . We also experience exactly the same "miracle" inside of ourselves: we can receive answers to any questions if we tune in to the right frequency. For "God" – the networked power and intelligence of the universe – is always present, surrounds us, cares for us, heals us, and provides us with the necessary information. Every step of the way, at every moment. None of us could exist otherwise. We are a part of the whole and from the whole we permanently receive the power and information that we need to "function correctly". "God's" frequencies (or for atheists: the frequencies of the cosmic database) are just as real as radio waves and other electromagnetic frequency fields, but here we do not have a technical device as a receiver. Instead we have ourselves. We, ourselves, have the sensory equipment that enables us to download and manifest the information, vibrations and energies that are necessary for healing.

The knowledge that can be tapped is endless and it is the basis for all living creatures. It is not only we who access this knowledge, the bat does so too, when it flies through ruins with ultrasound. How does a spider really build its web? It is not the spider's own intelligence at work; instead, it is its innate ability to access the knowledge that is necessary to build a web from the cosmic database that is at work. How do bees build their honeycombs and their state? There is not one single bee that could answer that question. They are connected with the cosmic database. How do people build embryos and their own children? Not a single human being – neither man nor woman – can answer this question. We are connected to the cosmic database. Life arose in the ocean. But how did it get onto land? This was an incredible act of evolution, when animals that were hungry for knowledge and that lived under water, had the unbending inner drive to crawl onto land. Like the people in Plato's allegory of the cave, who said: "We want to get out into the sun!" Beings are born with such inner driving forces, and they constitute a part of the inner potential form, the "entelechy" of the species. These reptiles thus had to perform a miracle; they had to create something that they could not communicate to anyone about, namely lungs. They had to be able to replace breathing through gills with breathing through lungs – what an "insane" project! Once this succeeded, there was a new "success model" for the development of life on earth. The new model entered, as information, into the body of information of the earth (the noosphere), and it had the effect of a force field for the further development.

Today, we find ourselves in a similar evolutionary leap with the corresponding field creation, when we try to orient our civilisation anew, develop new sources of energy, create new social systems, and provide new possibilities for a fulfilled love life between the sexes. Nobody could succeed in this if they had to do so alone. But we do not have to do it alone, for we are constantly cooperating with the universe by tuning in to and downloading the information and energies from the cosmic database that are necessary for this new leap in evolution. Once the leap has occurred successfully somewhere, it spreads on earth and a new "morphogenetic field" is created. All of evolution follows the principle of field creation through leaps (mutations). New evolutionary stages and new force fields always emerge from such leaps. A similar leap could now give human evolution a new direction. It can emerge as models in the centres of the future that we call "Healing Biotopes", "Peace Villages" or "Peace Research Villages". As soon as these first centres are functioning, they will have a global field effect.

When building its cultures, humanity was always dependent on accessing very specific information from the cosmic database. This information gave rise to force fields that created societies with belief systems that were shared by all, for example the belief that jealousy consitutes a part of love. They downloaded the information, according to which it seemed obvious that jealousy is a part of love. Today, we need to download other information, according to which it is even more obvious that jealousy is not a part of love. Furthermore, they downloaded information, according to which they could claim that war is a part of life. Today, we are at a point where we can say definitively: war is not a part of life, provided we use other information and higher patterns of order from the cosmic database. They downloaded information, according to which they believed that we need oil and other fossil fuels to cover our need for energy on earth. If we download other information we will discover entirely different possiblities for using solar energy, cosmic energy and other subtle energy fields.

Now comes the crucial point: what information we download depends on what vision we create and what direction we pay attention to. What do we focus our minds on? In situations of conflict, are we willing and able to focus our mind on the higher level of non-violence? In our love relationships, are we willing and able to focus our minds on the principle of a non-violent and sincere relationship between the sexes? Can we do so, even if two women love the same man? And if two men love the same woman? Are we able to do so in our vision? Do we have an image of love that is free of lies, free of the fear of being abandoned, free of clinging, and free of reproaches and possessiveness? Once this image has arisen in the hearts and minds of a few people, it has latently arisen in many hearts and minds, for we are a part of the whole. Today, we are at an historical point in time, when much depends on if we succeed in creating new fields in the core areas of our lives. If we succeed in solving, at a higher level, a conflict that up to now has remained unsolved, then we have created a model that immediately creates a field, for we are all mutually connected with the same frequency of information in our basic vibration, our genetic code, and our brain waves. We are all a part of the trans-individual body of information. We no longer have to be missionaries or try to convince anyone and we no longer need to go out and announce a new truth, for the field is operating all by itself.

We need a vision that enables us to integrate our lives on earth with the whole of the universe. Without this connection we will not really be able to download the right healing information. There is a pattern of order in the universe, which is inherent in all beings. It is the Sacred Matrix, and we must orient ourselves according to its rules. For this we have been researching and developing the life forms of the new centres for the last 30 years. Do we have a vision that aligns our earthly life with the order of the cosmic (divine) world? We will be able to hold the necessary vision on one condition: if a growing group of committed people, who are open to the world, declares itself willing to connect fully with the rules of the Sacred Matrix and to follow them in a binding way? This connection must be established in order for us to be able to access the healing information for the distressed areas of the earth, for Colombia, Palestine and other regions, but also for ourselves and our communities. We must work to keep replacing our habits of thinking and behaving by more clear (learnable) rules of behavior of the Sacred Matrix and the principles of the deepest form of non-violence in our own relationships. This connection between personal change and political peace work is obligatory in the holographic world view. It is only when a growing group of people enters into a process of constant self-correction that the new information can be downloaded. We cannot continue life as usual and tell our friends in San José in Colombia: "Sure, we will help you." The solution definitively lies on a different level. San José, and all other places on earth, all peoples and all communities are a part of the larger whole. Once they find their way to reconnect, they will share the power and the wisdom, the beauty and the intelligence, the love and the healing power of the greater whole. If they themselves are too shocked by the misery and distress, then other people must do it. Currently, this is the division of labour on earth. We have the freedom to learn what this reconnection with the larger whole looks like. The answers that we need for the healing of our relationships, our conflicts of love, our fears and illnesses - these answers are needed for the healing of all places on earth. The vision for healing, both our own healing and global healing, entails reintegrating our lives into the larger whole of the universe. This must no longer fail in the area of our most intimate issues. Once we no longer succumb to the innermost conflicts, which mostly lie in the area of love, because we can solve them at a new level of order, then we will have a world model.

We can stop dealing with the inner topics ideologically. The only possibility we have is to solve them ourselves. That is why Tamera is engaged in this great yearlong healing work that one cannot summarise and pass on during a brief summer university. We cannot tell the people in Colombia or Palestine or wherever: "You must live in free love, because otherwise it won't work." I am afraid that we did commit such sins of youth twenty years ago. Nor do we have to be able to do everything ourselves or have ready answers to all questions. As sure as this topic is an area of the Sacred Matrix, God will help us when we do what we already can, honestly, truthfully and courageously. That is enough. The Sacred Matrix is the greatest power that helps us when we open our connection to it.

The extent to which we access the power, intelligence, love and reconciliation of the divine world depends on how open our connection to it is. And that should be learned collectively. We need a world group of ten or thirty or a thousand people – the number is not important – that agrees on these issues, and we also need action groups within the various communities, here and at other places on earth, who have understood this. A political practice for the global healing of the earth must definitely be connected with a spiritual life practice, including the core areas of sex, love, partnership and community.

There is one phenomenon that comes to our aid when it comes to the healing work, and that is the self-healing powers of every organism. If I cut my finger, all my cells will work together to heal the wound. I see the universe as a living unified organism, the overall organism of the living world. All power, intelligence and information that is active in this organism is also active in all subordinate organisms, down to our own bodies. Every organism has access to the self-healing forces that are necessary to heal all injuries and illnesses, provided that we do not intervene and disrupt them. Instead of causing disruptions, we must understand and follow the self-healing forces. This is what is meant by following spiritual rules. A spiritual way of life means to live so that the self-healing forces of the world can increasingly impact our lives. There is nothing else that we need to do. The self-healing forces are always there, for they constitute a core part of our lives. We can always activate them for ourselves and others, provided that we download the suitable energies from the cosmic matrix.

We humans are organs of the whole; we share in its wisdom, its omnipotence and its healing power. Let us together regain this way of seeing the human being, which was a matter of course in the highly developed cultures of ancient archaic history. Otherwise, no circles of stones and no Maltese temples could have been built. It was destroyed during the patriarchal and imperialist era, and today it is re-awakened and re-activated through the reconnection with the female sources of creation. Once we reconnect with the knowledge that there is a universal, cosmic sacred "operating system", also on earth, which functions differently from the current operating system of human society, then the questions arises which operating system we wish to connect to. The real "holy land" will emerge wherever the divine order shines through in the structures of real non-violent cooperation between human beings and all fellow creatures. This can occur in the Healing Biotopes and the true peace villages, the centres of the future, the models of a new creation on earth.

Every new thought structure changes the structure of matter. Every new set of information gives rise to new molecular structure in the body of the whole, also in the genetic code. New synapses and new neural paths are created in the brain and new energy paths are created in the body. These energies, which so far were imprisoned in our bodies and could not find a way out, are suddenly free to move. We must think this through to the end, extending it to the social and technological structures that we need for the world of the future, and not only for the parts of the world which we address now to be in distress, for the whole world is in distress. Let us look at this earth from this larger perspective and from a distance, and let us carry out the mission that we are here for.

Part 2: The Theory in Detail

THE WORLD AS A HOLOWAVE

The universe is a living unit. All things contained in the world are engaged in a mutual, coherent evolution. Anything that occurs spreads as a holo-wave through space and time. Whatever occurs at one place is happening everywhere (in corresponding translation and at different scales). No star can burn out without something changing on earth. Every event of war and every event of love leave behind traces in the more subtle tissue of the biosphere. World matter that is being nudged somewhere, vibrates everywhere. The world reacts to each and every event, from the molecular structures to the galaxies, and from a delicate thought to the most complex systems of information. What we are doing right now can save a human life far away or else it can create interference and conflict elsewhere.

Each thought, each action, derives from a current in the world matter. Everything that manifests somewhere on earth emerges from the invisible waves of the great whole. We are not only receivers of world matter, but also its activists and its control organs. With each action and with each thought, something is being changed in the world matter. If only we were successful in building up complex information for peace at any one place in the world, a truly non-violent community, that also has the ability to withstand opposing forces, then this information can affect the entire noosphere of our planet. The Project of the Healing Biotopes emerged from such thoughts. The more such places (acupuncture points) are developed, the tighter the ring for global peace will become.

The world is an oscillating continuum. What we see in massacres and wars are global oscillations that may show up in other places in a much more subtle manner. Global life on earth, including all psychic events, is a continuum of frequencies. Nobody is uninvolved. Whatever is present in well protected, affluent families in the form of disappointed love, secret lies and latent aggression erupts in other places in the form of hatred and genocide. Newly created peace and reconciliation sends vibrations into the world circle that arrive everywhere. We no longer live in an era of matter, but in an era of frequency. Spiritual and psychic vibrations are of a more penetrating nature than material forces.

This perspective opens up a totally new picture for the possibility of healing our planet. It is a matter of entering the correct frequencies in the whole. According to the quantum physicist David Bohm, between ten and a hundred coherently oscillating people can change humankind as a whole.

THE IMAGE

The image is that of an organism attacked by an illness that shows up in many sick places. An intelligent doctor does not treat each place separately, but instead treats the whole organism. Applied to the global situation of our time, this means that an intelligent concept not only provides peace work for special places of crisis, but also concentrates on the healing of the global organism, of both human being and earth. The problem is not only that thousands of individual areas are ill. The whole needs an "injection" and a new energy. The noosphere needs new information. The nuclei of the cells need a new impetus to be able to send fresh steering impulses to the organisms.

FIVE KEY STATEMENTS

First: The entire earth and all of humanity form an integrated organism, a holistic system, which reacts as a whole to the healing impulses that are injected.

Second: The key information of a new, non-violent code of life is directed to the inner sphere of community, truth, trust, love, Eros and religion. The bifurcations, from where the course of human evolution on earth takes new directions - as soon as the material prerequisites are fulfilled -, lie in the inner realm of the human being.

Third: Peace work is healing work. Central to it is the building up of trust. If someone asks what peace means, then the answer is that peace is trust. Trust between human beings, trust between lovers, trust between parents and children, young people and adults, trust between women who love the same man, trust between men who love the same woman, trust between nations, trust between the human being and animals, the human being and nature, and the human being and the world. The deepest meaning lies in finding the code of trust. Healing Biotopes are places, where the conditions that can support the emergence and the growth of perpetual trust are created consciously.

Fourth: Neither moral appeals, individual conversions nor individual spiritual exercise will produce the necessary change. Instead, new communitarian and societal structures must be developed to promote a continuous growth of truth, trust and solidarity.

Fifth: Communities of the future, which will create the new structures of the inner sphere of human beings, will produce a global field effect. As a result of the functioning of holistic systems, a new code of life will change planetary life.

All five statements are self-evident.

The *first* one concerns the planetary bio-system as an integrated organism. This is confirmed by biological systems theories, such as Lovelock's Gaia Hypothesis and the theory of the "biological internet", which claims that all beings are connected through the frequencies of their cellular nuclei (DNA), and which we could call "hypercommunication" or "basic communication". The genetic code of all beings has the same basic mathematical structure, i.e. all beings follow the same basic information of life. They all live within an integrated body of information or, as Teilhard de Chardin put it, in an integrated "noosphere".

The *second* statement is the result of the inner logic of peace work: peace in the outer world corresponds to the degree that peace has been established in the inner world. We need a new code of life that replaces fear with trust, separation with participation, and ideology with insight. In the centre of this new code lies a new relationship between the sexes, one which is capable of creating lasting experiences of love and a permanent connection between sexual power and personal relationship. For this we need a good communal and spiritual anchor. The main point is ultimately to overcome the fear of separation, mistrust and mutual deception in love, one of the most intimate areas of human life. **There can be no peace on earth as long as there is war in love.**

The *third* statement deals with healing. This statement speaks for itself. Where there is trust, fear is overcome. Where fear has disappeared, violence is overcome. Trust is a true tonic for healing.

The *fourth* statement is determined by history. There have always been individuals like Jesus, Mahatma Gandhi, Etty Hillesum, Jacques Lusseyran or Martin Luther King, who have reached a high level of purity and divine power, although it is doubtful whether this has made the world a better place. Individual purification is necessary. However, it must find its anchor in a new collective structure, or else it will not have a permanent effect vis-à-vis the overpowering force of violence. Gandhi said: "Be the change you want to see in the world". Yes! We need new social entities whose structures are suitable for generating a maximum of human beings who can live according to Gandhi's talk.

The *fifth* statement arises from the first one. If new information, a new vibration or a new direction of force is input into an integrated organism, these become effective in all its parts. If the input is made at a few points, or at only one acupuncture point, then it will have an effect in terms of a resulting field of force within the entire organism. An analogy between the human body and the body of the earth and the body of humankind appears to be permissible.

CREATING NEW FIELDS OF INFORMATION

The code of global healing contains new information. Old chains of information of war, jealousy, fear and violence, which over the centuries have constantly been accessed and activated, must be dissolved and replaced by new ones. Life itself is built on information. The fate of humans and all co-creatures depends on which information is accessed. Nothing is written in stone, and almost every matrix can be realised if the corresponding information is activated (see Chapter 3).

We live in a real multiverse with an infinite number of latent "parallel universes". We can also call them parallel holograms. There are holograms of fear and holograms of trust, holograms of alienation and holograms of connection. Which ones of the many possibilities manifest in our lives and bodies depends on the information that we extract from the world and on the information that we input into the world. (This can be understood much easier if one applies it to a love relationship.) We do not react to reality, but to our interpretation of it, i.e. to the information that we have about reality.

The theory of global healing is based on a concept of information. Information is not a material, but a mental-spiritual quantity. What does "information" and "field of information" mean?

If you are angry at someone because he or she has done something wrong, and if you then receive information that it was not that person who had done it, then the anger immediately disappears. Your relationship to this person changes within a second. It is information that leads to this change. Your entire emotional system listens to a single piece of information. It is information that controls the flow of life. Information controls the entire living world.

If dealing with information that is not of an everyday nature, but constitutes entirely new fundamental information about your life or about processes in the world, then your entire life will probably change all at once. Let us go one step further and translate this to humanity as a whole. If collective information is developed that puts humanity's collective belief system on a fully new track, then humanity will be facing a new field of its own future. The task is to create collective information that gives evolution a new direction. Collective information changes the collective flow of life and gives it a new direction. How a being, a community or humanity grows depends on the information that is input into that entity. In this sense information is of basic biological importance for all living beings (and is there anything that is not alive?)

Whether we will find a peaceful re-connection with the whole or not depends on if we succeed in erasing the dogma of partriarchal religion, which opposes love, replacing it with the more friendly information of a Marian Age.

We live in a holographic world. All information of the world is available and can be retrieved at any one point. Theoretically, the overall world information can be "downloaded" at any place, at any given point and with the needed frequency. Radiaesthesia, kinesiology and other methods, which we have examined thoroughly, are based on the omnipresence of all necessary information. It is possible to tap into the world information or certain fields of it, such as the field of mathematics or music. We all know the phenomena of so-called child prodigies. These children have musical or mathematical abilities that by far surpass our imagination. Although these children mostly do not have a special intelligence, they seem to have some sort of antenna with which they connect to parts of the universal database in a special way. We had a guest staying with us who was able to continuously produce Goethe-type poems without ever having studied Goethe. For some reason he was connected to a "Goethe field". There is a man living in England with a low IQ, who, when sitting at a piano is able to play 50 pieces of classical music free of any mistakes. He is obviously connected to a field of music. People like Houdini, clairvoyants and other mediums, some mental healers, yogis, circus acrobats and people engaged in extreme sports all have PSI capabilities. PSI does not conform to traditional notions of our physical world. These people are connected to information that lies beyond that described by conventional physics. World information, whether known or unknown, is everywhere.

No spider could build its web without being connected to the corresponding field of information from the cosmic database. No ant colony and no bee hive could be created if it were not connected to the corresponding field of information – with the queen as the "web-master".

Furthermore, no jealousy, no revenge and no fear could exist if there were no collective fields of information for them. What we see as natural reactions, natural reflexes or instincts are the effects of collective fields of information, which at a given time affect a given population that is at a given state of development. These are not spiritual, biological or physical natural laws that always apply. They apply so long as the corresponding fields of information predominate. They become invalid as soon as new, different information from the cosmic database is accessed. Just as the anger about an accused person immediately dissipates as soon as we receive information about his or her innocence.

The totality of possibilities is unlimited. The world is full of latent – and mostly unused – fields of information. Some of them have a special power of attraction; we call them "attractor fields". If we come close to such fields, we become restless or else we become alive and full of expectation. Some "numinous" power attracts us. Such attractor fields determine our longings, our preferences and our goals in life, whether consciously or subconsciously. Emotional-psychological attractor fields are inner force fields in which archetypal patterns of the collective unconscious become active. Such archetypal figures are for example "the Warrior", the "Priest", the "Messiah", the "Great Mother" (Nossa Senora, Notre Dame), the "Empire", the "Holy Land", the "Community", "Good", "Beauty" and "Power". Needless to say, Eros is one of the strongest attractor fields. Since our lives are permanently – usually subconsciously - influenced by such attractor fields, it makes sense to create and send out the information into the world that is suitable for accessing or creating powerful and yet non-violent attractor fields from the cosmic database.

The world is charged with invisible energies and information that operate everywhere and that we are not aware of because we cannot perceive them directly.

At this very moment and in this room, there are radio waves from broadcasting stations worldwide, as well as radio waves from all the galaxies of the universe. I only have to switch on the radio and go to a certain wavelength in order to call up information. The same is true of television and the internet : what is invisible but present in space can become visible, for instance in the form of a picture or written words. Marvel over marvel! The invisible world is full of information and frequencies. Were we without receivers, we would know nothing about it!!!

The same is true for the firing power of wood. If we did not have a match to ignite it, we would not know about its firing power. The difference between the empirical world and the real possibilities that it harbours is enormous. Now apply this to people.

An enormous invisible world full of possibilities is always present. We only have to find the small shift in consciousness in order to call it up.

How and why can the new healing information be spread globally? The answer can be found in the special functioning of holistic systems. Information that is compatible with the system and that is input into it, is effective in all its part (see the above analogy about sick organisms). All parts are connected with each other through frequencies and are in resonance with each other. Humanity, together with the whole of the biosphere, is a holistic system. What I do to animals has an effect on people, and what I do to human beings has an effect on animals. The basic life structure is the same in all beings (example: DNA). All beings are part of "one being" and "one consciousness". Frequencies, information and energies are all connected with each other in a continuous cycle. Together, they form a biological internet with radio contact occurring between all participants. This, according to Sheldrake, gives rise to such phenomena as "thought transference" and "morphogenetic field creation." When an impulse that is input into this radio communication contains core information, a field-like change occurs that makes itself noticed either as a "mutation", an "evolutionary leap" or a "transformation". Such transformation occurs in the lives of individuals as well as in the lives of entire populations. All of evolution seems to have taken place through the impact of such field-like mutations. If we are successful in effecting a change in the nucleus of the areas of love, trust, sexuality and community, then this will call forth a marked change of direction in human evolution.

(As an aside: The development of positive alternatives in the core areas would have an unforeseeable impact on outer conditions. A society with a fulfilled love life and functioning communities would no longer be dependent on vicarious satisfaction through consumption, property, power and war. The destruction of nature is in the service of a civilisation that is dependent on vicarious satisfaction, because it has blocked the elementary flow of life energies. The development of functioning planetary communities, in which the elementary needs of belonging, having a home, of connection are fulfilled, would then have a fundamental ecological healing effect. I am convinced that we will experience this global development concretely during this current 21st century. The healing thoughts regarding the ecological, social, sexual and spiritual areas are intimately connected with each other.)

The procreation of new systems occurs through "contagion" and resonance. Everywhere on earth we see the phenomenon of "contagion". For that we need neither bacteria nor other material vectors. If one of two similar systems is changed, the probability is high that the change will devolve to the other one as well. The systems "infect" each other, even if they are separated from each other through barriers of glass or quartz. The systems infect each other mutually.

This phenomenon is known in physics, chemistry and biology and we know it even better amongst people. A simple example: If one person starts to cough during a lecture, many others start to cough right away. A latent cough field creates the chain reaction. A more encompassing example: If the youth of the western world has an existential crisis and a philosopher like Sartre or Camus expresses this crisis, then hundreds of thousands of young people in Germany and France read the literature of existentialism. When a new field of thought emerges in physics, for example the concept of the quantum, within a short period of time the "quantum theory" is developed and it will not take long until it is accepted by all physicists. When the first graffiti artists left their wonderful figures on the walls, we soon saw the same figures in all big cities, underground stations and bridge pillars of the world, from New York to Tokyo. Keep these examples in mind! Why do the same figures suddenly appear in the same perfection on the walls of ruins in the remote Portuguese province of Alentejo?

If a latent field for a new action, a new development or a change occurs in a population, then this latent field can change into

visible reality as soon as the first elements do. **As soon as the first cells of humankind are able to develop new systems for a free life and build up functioning communities, the field will spread on earth and come into visible reality at many places.**

If one has understood this part, then the logical core of our Political Theory has been understood. The further explanations serve to illustrate the theory.

STEERING OF POWER

Fascism, which ceased being a part of public propaganda with the downfall of Hitler's empire, has become a worldwide phenomenon again. It was, after all, not only the one man Hitler but millions of people who had nothing else in mind but to escape the narrowness of their lives by exerting violence. This can be seen as the psychological background of all wars that are being fought today, regardless of capitalism or communism, Milosevic or Putin. The goal is to finally mean something in this world, to finally feel power and get even for what one has suffered oneself.

The less human energies feel at home in love and trust, the more they turn toward systems of political, technical and military might. Wars are not the result of the natural laws of life, but of blocked and redirected energies. The emotional and psychological energies must be given a new direction where they can connect with the lives of our co-creatures, instead of fighting them. The principle of worldwide healing consists of new control systems for the bio-energetic, emotional and psychological energies on earth.

The power coming from the universe passes through the relay stations of human beings and through the structures that they have built. There, the power is led into new paths. For them to be healing paths, the mechanism has to be recognised and corrected by new information. Only one pre-condition is needed for this to occur: a sufficient number of human beings have to agree on the direction and goal of the new paths. The new centres, which will be developed as part of the plan of the Healing Biotopes, will be places where these paths become visible through research and studies, through new experiences, and through international cooperation.

We have said that information controls the life processes and the directions of flow of life energies. Human society is a control system of cosmic and human energies. The control of the available energy and whether this leads to fortune or misfortune depends largely on the mental, social and technological control systems that a culture develops. Streams of energy can be led to collide with each other, resulting in paralysis, fear, enmity, violence and psychosomatic illnesses (the sexual urge collides with morals, obedience collides with rebellion). Equally, the streams of energy can be steered in such a way as to harmonise with each other, thereby producing healing, love and cooperation on a higher and larger plane. The world needs new steering systems for the steering and healing of the energies contained in world matter. New steering systems mean new information systems, new systems of thought, new concepts for life, and new systems for cooperation with the developing forces of life.

The technological aspect is important. In order to end the destruction of the environment, we need new systems of energy. The search for functioning methods to capture free cosmic energy could soon make a significant contribution. Before this occurs, special solar technologies will be adopted, such as those that have been developed by the technology group around Jürgen Kleinwächter in Lörrach/Germany.

More important are the mental, sexual and psycho-social aspects of energy control. It is primarily the distorted psychic energies world-wide that need new steering. During the thousands of years of patriarchal cultural tradition, the switch that regulates the innermost energies has been set to slow down and divert them. It has to be turned up again, until the stream of energy is in order again and can flow freely. We need a new code to dismantle old blocks. We need higher levels of energy in order to transform the existing chaos. New energy supplies, so called "dissipative structures" are formed that can re-establish the energetic balance on a higher level of order. Ilya Prigogine received the Nobel Prize for the discovery of this principle. He made his discovery in a chemistry lab, but it can be applied to human conditions. Existing conflicts can only be solved at a higher level of order. The energies of conflicts that have so far been unresolved can "escape upwards" and can reassemble in new structures of order. There could, for example, be a higher structure of order in which the love between two persons and free love merge, or a higher level where the conflict between individualism and collectivism disappears. As we know through 30 years of research work in communities, this higher pattern of order truly exists.

Once such a connection has occurred successfully, it displays a morphogenetic effect: the new pattern of order, the newly acquired form, is effective in the whole of the holon as a new field of information, which again will generate many analogue forms.

Higher levels of order are a higher form of being in union. Forces, directions of development, people and groups that previously confronted each other with indifference or hostility, can – if new energies and information are added – connect anew and befriend each other. Whether we have a positive or negative approach towards the world, towards people and towards our fellow creatures, is a question of information and energy.

Equally, it is a question of information and energy whether we react with anger or with joy to the new impulses that change our lives.

COMMUNITY

The new levels of order exist in new forms of community and in an *encompassing* cooperation with our fellow beings in nature. Higher forms of union are higher forms of consciousness. In my opinion, it is no longer possible to find the basic information and core forces for a healthy world without focusing all research on the development and creation of complex communities.

Thirty years of community work - such as the **Project of the Healing Biotopes** – reveal, perhaps more than anything else, the depth needed for a paradigm shift to occur in the human sphere. The new code of life is a result of functioning communities, communities in which the usual conflicts of authority, recognition, money, sex and love can finally be dissolved in favour of humane structures of truth, transparency and mutual support.

The global concept of healing starts with the concrete development of functioning communities. This has obviously proven to be more difficult than any development of ion weapons and genetic engineering. Instead, people have been waiting for the Messiah to come to release them. However, the Messiah does not exist. But a communitarian intelligence capable of developing the code of healing does exist.

We live in a time of actual transformation. To use Ernst Bloch´s words, it is a time of "utopian latency". New possibilities that truly exist in the information chains of the emergent universe are pushing to be realised.

Humankind has waged war for thousands of years and was excited by slogans and guns. The liturgies of violence are repeated again and again, from Homer to Hollywood. The same patterns, the same chains of information in the genetic code, the same synapses in the brain, and the same hormones have been activated again and again, and the same slogans have been shouted and passed on to the next generations. They were incorrect, unexamined basic axioms of thinking that led to the globalisation of cruelty, male axioms of law and order, sexual suppression, sinful bodies and a punishing God.

The one-sided selection of information in favour of power, war and repression led to astonishing achievements in the technical area and at the same time to a return of the pre-cultural mental, ethical and emotional structures of robbery. "High Tech in War and Neanderthal in Love" – this is the cultural image of today's civilisation.

Let us imagine where humankind would be today if it had used the intelligence at its disposal for love instead of war! A civilisation that has produced self-navigating weapons and that can bring electronic labs to Mars would also be capable of creating completely new social systems in which violence and lies no longer provide an evolutionary advantage and where love is no longer linked to jealousy. It is not the nature of human beings that destroyed our planet, but the one-sided choice of our possibilities. We can no longer react to all this with accusations and anger. The earth does not need our reactions and emotions but our intelligence.

(Further information about the issue of community can be found in Chapter 11 and in the book "The Sacred Matrix" Publisher's note.)

THE RULES OF LIFE OF TAMERA

The Project of the Healing Biotopes was initiated in order to find and develop this code. Our research work was always strongly connected to the development of the community and all the corresponding human issues. Non-violent structures, social transparency, mutual support, truth in contact, solidarity in sexuality and love: these are not empty words, they constitute a binding orientation for the concrete lives of all participants.

Life in Tamera is based on a kind of "rules of the order". They contain the following 12 points:

1. You are in a place of research for healing and for peace work. Behave in such a way that your life serves both healing and peace.

2. Become a witness of your thoughts. Talk, think and act in such a way as to generate peace within you, then peace will also be generated in others.

3. Sound is pure information, and a new culture needs a new sound. Therefore, do not make unnecessary noise and stay in contact and resonance with "the Whole".

4. Central to the ethics of Tamera are three basic rules:
   First: Truth, and this also applies to love.
   Second: Mutual support.
   Third: Responsible participation in the community.

5. If you lie to each other or disguise yourselves in front of each other you are becoming an accomplice of global war. Study and follow the laws of transparency and truth. "At the heart of truth, all fear disappears." (Lichtenfels: Sources of Love and Peace)

6. It does not serve peace to suppress sexual attraction. In Tamera you have the chance to deal with this in an unobtrusive and thankful way and to learn how the game works. Shyness is not a sin.

7. You have no right to possess others, including your partner or your children. They do not belong to us, they belong to the world.

8. There is no tenure when it comes to love and sexuality. In Tamera you are exposed to a different erotic culture. Do not demand of anyone that they fulfil your own wants and needs. Eros is not a legal entity but a true gift.

9. Tamera does not promote fast contacts and quick sexual fulfilment. Take your time and understand what is meant by free sexuality. Study the intellectual/spiritual basic thoughts of the project.

10. The power lies in the mind. The paradigm shift that is necessary for a new culture to emerge requires continuous mental/ spiritual work. Participation in "Monte Cerro" requires attendance at the regular SD-forum and a daily mental/spiritual hour. Full time students are obliged to take part in all training events.

11. All beings and fellow creatures are aspects of one's own life. What we do unto them, will fall back on ourselves. Therefore, treat them with care and never torment an animal.

12. Learn to build up energy within yourself and to conserve it. Never act from affect.

Chapter 6

Five Key Thoughts

(Speech without notes about the previous chapter, held in January, 2006)

I will once again begin with the image.
An organism is infected by an illness and shows signs of illness in many places.
This organism is the earth, humanity, every community and every individual body.
A wise doctor does not treat every individual place, but the entire organism. Applied to the global situation of our times, this means that a wise concept for peace not only deals with peace work in special areas of suffering, but with the healing of the global organism of the human being and the earth.

These are the five key thoughts:
1. The entire earth and all of humanity constitute one unified organism, i.e. a holistic system, a holon, which reacts as a whole whenever a corresponding force, information, or healing power is input.
The organism of the earth and humanity reacts as a whole. What does this really mean? How is it possible that something can be felt on Tahiti if we do something here in Portugal? In order to understand this thought, we must first find the image of the whole again. Then we will notice that it this is the same question as: "How is it possible that I think something in my head and then my stomach no longer hurts?" Or else I introduce an acupuncture needle somewhere on my body and the pain in my knees disappears. How is this possible? The connections are the same. It is good to first of all allow ourselves to be awed by this, for we are dealing with the miracle of a holistic system. We can see the miracle of our Political

Theory, the miracle that we call morphogenetic field creation, at work in our own bodies, our own organism. One single thought at the right time can change my whole inner life. How is it possible that a single thought can change how I am when I am doing the dishes, when interacting with my beloved, when studying, when dealing with money, etc? One single cardinal peace thought, such as "I do not have to impress anyone", "I will not be judged", "I no longer have to lie", or "I can step out of this damned old prison", taking one single such thought to its conclusion, can change one's entire inner life. One single central shift in the co-existence between human beings, occurring somewhere on earth, can at least stimulate the collective subconscious, or rather the hyper-conscious of all of humanity, so that with some probability the same shift, the same change, can occur at many other places. Look at the analogies! This is what I mean when I say that we have to keep entering a state of silence in order to see things calmly. The connections that are described in the Political Theory when dealing with field creation are shown to us in our own bodies and everywhere in nature.

2. The core information of a new, non-violent life code lies in the inner area of community, truth, trust, love, Eros and religion. Once the material prerequisites are fulfilled, the determinant points (bifurcations) from where human evolution on earth takes on a new direction lie within the human being.

If we go to places of suffering on earth we see that aid initially consists of fulfilling material needs and providing outer security, just as Ibrahim Abouleish has done in the Egyptian desert in Sekem or as Bunker Roy has done at Barefoot College in Tilonia in India. But as soon as the outer conditions are fulfilled, one will notice that the crucial points when it comes to creating a non-violent culture on earth can be found inside. Gorbachev once said: "Fear must disappear from the earth." But fear cannot disappear, so long as it is encapsulated like a tubercle in our cells and our souls. Inside there, in the sexual and spiritual areas of life, we find the point where healing must occur. A global field can be created for this bifurcation, for example through our current work.

3. Peace work is healing work. At its centre lies the establishment of trust. If someone asks what peace really is, the answer is: peace is TRUST.

A friend of ours, who has been engaged in peace work in the Balkans for many years, wrote us a letter saying that he doesn't really know what peace is. He does not know it, because he is missing the experience of trust. Peace can then only be defined as the absence of war. But when we give negative definitions to a positive story, this is just like saying: "I do not know what it is about." Trust is an experience. Trust may be the deepest human experience of all. If night-long discussions were to make it possible for true trust to develop between the new Hamas government and Israeli politicians, or if it could be created from the outside, then we would have an entirely different kind of lever to influence the drama in the Middle East.

Trust between people, between lovers – between life partners! Those are the depths of the concept of the Healing Biotopes and the new centres on earth. Trust between men who love the same woman, trust between men who love the same man, trust between peoples, trust between humans and animals, for example spiders, rats, snakes, and dogs! Trust between humans and nature, also when storms are brewing, trust between humans and the world. Deep down it is a matter of finding the code of trust. Healing biotopes are places where conscious work is carried out to create the conditions necessary for the emergence and growth of permanent trust. This sets the stage for the healing process.

4. It is not moral appeals, individual transformation and spiritual exercises that bring about the necessary changes. Instead, it is communal and societal structures that have yet to be created that will make it possible for truth, trust and solidarity to develop and gain permanence. This is a very important point and it is so new

that nobody understands it at first. One hears the words but one hardly senses what they mean.

One greatly prefers the messages by Aurobindo or Sai Baba, Claude AnShin Thomas or Peace Pilgrim, Prentice Mulford or Jesus of Nazareth. But these messages are always addressed to the individual. Read the Sermon on the Mount and the 10 Commandments, visit the spiritual communities of our time, and you will notice that the messages are always addressed to the individual. It is always the individual who is given the advice to meditate, to practice truth, humility and love of one's neighbour. But these commandments cannot be followed, because the individual is living in societal conditions under which they cannot be followed. Also, while the spiritual principles of life, as they are presented in many books or workshops cannot be doubted, nor can they be realised within existing structures. If we wish to re-integrate the sanctity of the world into our lives, we need new structures in society. That is the definitive insight after 5 000 years of war on earth.

We need a different logical form of message. We need a message that has a collective quality to it. This has absolutely nothing to do with uniform collectivism or communism, on the contrary. The new message is of course also directed at the individual, for we want to change and have to change in order for healing to be able to occur in ourselves. But for this change to become permanent it must be anchored in new social, ethical and ecological structures. We need new life structures for all those involved. We need new structures of community, so that very many individuals can have the possibility to find trust again. Or a fulfilled love life. Or a feeling of home and belonging.

One must understand what it means to be working to develop structures, to develop a container in which healing forces can come together and be passed on to the outside. Free love is a part of this container. Free love, free sexuality – in friendship and trust. That is not a moral appeal that is addressed to individuals. Instead, it means building a humane social system, in which it is possible to live the truth within Eros. This liberates the people from always having to lie secretly. Through this, they can become "good" in an ethical sense. Then they can follow the commandment: "Thou shalt not lie." If we do not create this structure, then we appeal to the individual to "Please stop lying", but we retain the reason for the lie. Many married couples have to lie to each other because they are not allowed to admit to each other their longing for other partners. Then they also have to see to it that neither of them notices anything. What a terrible situation! On top of it all comes the commandment: "Thou shalt not lie." It is enough to plunge you into moral despair and give up.

Here, it is not enough to enter the silence or to eat macrobiotic food. We have to create the concrete conditions and structures that make it possible for the participants in a community or society to become healthy, truthful people. This development has been ongoing in Tamera for several years. One cannot say much about it; instead, it must be experienced.

If you understand this point, then you can participate fully in the Project of the Healing Biotopes. A community that understands this point knows what it is doing. That is the alternative to every kind of therapy, and that is no exaggeration. The fortune or misfortune of humanity depends on whether it will be possible to establish functioning communities, in which truth becomes possible again, especially truth around topic Number One. As I have already mentioned, if truth becomes possible at this level, and when the cleansing process in the soul and mind begins at this level, then one soon arrives at the point where one also wants to cleanse oneself bodily. Now we have the go-ahead. Now I no longer have to eat, smoke, drink, etc. out of frustration.

I will now attempt to illustrate the logical structure involved. Those who have not solved their conflicts in love and who are not aware of any of this, will live a life in the latent stranglehold of collective conflicts that one cannot solve on one's own. They will not notice it, for the whole world is caught in this stranglehold and nobody will be different from anyone else. The efforts that one makes to get a healthy body, a healthy mind and a healthy spirituality will then be of a compensatory quality. At some point one will break down under such efforts, because what is unresolved is stronger. There is no higher power than that of sexuality and love, for we exist as man and woman. As long as that is not resolved, we are at the mercy of this power. Subconsciously, this world power is always the director. We remain more or less its puppets. It is Eros that controls human history from its innermost core. Society has a secret nervous system, which immediately reacts to the issues of this innermost topic. You can take any office as an example: as soon as it becomes known that something is going on in this area for any given person, everybody speaks about it. There is then hardly anything else other than this story that is interesting. Topic Number One is Topic Number One. At some point one renounces all ideologies and sees that this is truly so. But initially you are totally on your own with this discovery. If you want to talk to others about it, you first run into solid walls. This happened to the young Swiss doctor and author Fritz Zorn, who described his story in his touching book "Mars". That is why we need communities, so that more and more people can speak the truth in this area and at the same time can develop a life perspective that gives them fulfillment.

The creation of truth is a communitarian enterprise. The creation of trust is a communitarian project. The creation of a loving and sincere sexuality is a task for a functioning community. This constitutes the foundation of the Project of Healing Biotopes. Ever more seekers should know about this. Let us look around and network and see who the people are who are receptive to this message today.

5. The communities of the future that will be creating the new structures for the inner areas of the human being will have a global field effect. As a result of the functioning of holistic systems, a new code of life will change life on the planet. That is the core statement of the Political Theory. (It has been presented in detail in Chapter 5). I have repeatedly tried to portray the biosphere, includ-

ing the human being, as a unified body and organism, with a unified existence and consciousness. I have said that it is the same universal consciousness that weaves and vibrates and connects all things. Of course all spiritually awakened people say so, too.

It is interesting that in the meantime the same type of thoughts are also coming from science, from Lynn Margulis and James Lovelock and now also from many others, such as Grazyna Fosar and Franz Bludorf in their interesting book about "Networked Intelligence".

Slowly, people on earth are beginning to agree that the earth and its biosphere constitute a unified organism. The form of a seashell is a code of the universal flow of consciousness. Our organism is an imprint of world knowledge. The structure of our brains, the neural structure, and the structure of the nervous system are codes that have emerged from world knowledge. These are wonderful connections. It is the immediate perception that Goethe spoke about in his story about the leaf and the original plant. This kind of immediate mental-spiritual view teaches us how incredible the connections of Creation truly are, if one only can be quiet and simply look. We always have this course in miracles within us and around us as a latent possible insight. Because this is so, because all things are connected in this overall fabric of life, and because there is a unified noosphere or a unified body of information, information that has been input at any one point has an effect in all parts of the world. If this information concerns a core part of life, it has an even greater effect. And if it is held by a sufficiently high number of people, if it has developed a certain power, vitality and maturity, then its effect is even greater. When a critical point is reached, the real bifurcation of the overall life on our planet begins. We will know more about this in 20 years.

All 5 statements are self-evident.

But has the content been understood? Do I have any idea why a seed produces a eucalyptus tree? Do I know approximately what an entelechial core is, and what entelechy means? From what kind of a code do the forms of material life emerge? Aristotle called it entelechy, the inner target gestalt or potential form. And he knew nothing about the genetic code. At some point the question arises: could such a principle not also apply to human beings, to human society and to the development of mankind? There we have the deep statements by Sabine Lichtenfels, which are contained in her two books "Temple of Love" and "Dream Stones". They contain the deciphering of the stone circles at Évora and the old temples on the islands of Malta and Gozo. The stone circle is the legacy of a highly developed human society that existed for a long time on earth, before disappearing some 6,000 or 7,000 years ago. The people who lived then had great knowledge about love and community, about raising and educating children, about natural beings and about the interaction between the earthly and the cosmic worlds. They left behind this stone circle as a message about the basic pattern of a human community. Here, we speak of the "prehistoric utopia" or the "entelechial core" of human society. In this connection it is good to know that on our hill here in Tamera, a stone circle is being constructed with excavators and anything at our disposal, bringing us closer to what used to be conscious knowledge about the entelechial core of humanity. We are dealing with an inner basic pattern, not the repetition of an old structure.

Behind all these transitory aspects of history, we can discover the universal, perhaps eternal pattern, including our own, inner universal pattern. These are great, wonderful connections. I am grateful that we have the privilege of being a part of this development.

Chapter 7

The Parable of the Nut

(Excerpt from a lecture without notes at the Summer University 2005 in Tamera)

In this lecture I will often use the word "dream".

I am grateful that during the last few days we have heard about the "dream" that I am talking about from so many different directions. I thank Max Lindegger for his poetic relationship to nature, for how he sees and senses the dream of a landscape and for thereby giving us many very important practical suggestions for our landscape design. I thank Jürgen Kleinwächter for his great dream of the solar age. During this Summer University, we could also sense the dreams of the source provided by indigenous peoples. Of course we could also sense the misery and despair on earth that results from the suppression of this dream.

The Project of the Healing Biotopes is based on a global vision. In this global vision, all dreams are combined in the right way. There is a criteria for answering the questions: "What is right?" and "What is not right?" This criteria has nothing to do with our feelings or preferences. It would require an extra seminar to discuss these connections and the concepts of the Political Theory.

As I see it, the idea of the Healing Biotopes is of an historical dimension, just like the idea of agriculture or animal husbandry was during the Stone Age ten thousand years ago. Or the idea of elecricity during the 19th century. Such ideas usher in a new human civilisation. Human civilisation begins with global ideas. The thought of a globally encompassing idea came to me when I was studying cybernetics and it was reinforced through the study of holography.

The idea of Healing Biotopes conforms to an historical cycle, in which the evolution of the earth and humanity finds itself. The history of the human being is cyclical. We are at the end of a male oriented era of domination; we can call it the imperial age. We are also at the beginning of a new era that Jürgen Kleinwächter calls the solar age. In Tamera we sometimes speak of the "Marian" cultural era. We can say that not only individuals, but our whole planet is pregnant with a new birth.

For this pregnancy I would like to present the parable of a nut. I see a nut on a tree. It has a green nutshell. In it lies its core. One could say that this nut is pregnant with its core. The core is still covered. The great physicist David Bohm spoke of the hidden or implicit order, in which the real world exists. This is the latent world with its latent possibilities that now wants to germinate. The world where the germination has already manifested is the revealed or explicit order.

The inner part of the nut thus reveals itself at the proper time. We then experience a revelation. Before, we only saw the green nutshell. But suddenly it opens and something emerges from within, something unseen and unexpected to human eyes. It is only conceivable, detectable and comprehensible for divine antennae. It is something totally different from what this nutshell led us to believe – it is the nut. The same is true for a chestnut. This is a fascinating parable. As a child I was obsessed by this discovery. When it was time to harvest the nuts, I got up as early as possible and wandered around the farms to see if there were any more nuts on the ground. Or chestnuts.

The phenomenon of revelation or unveiling accompanied me until I noticed, when I was an adult, that it also had to do with sexuality, with Eros. I suddenly understood the meaning of the veil in the Orient and the revelation that one experiences in the process of unveiling. I believe that this is a universal parable of nature. When the time is ripe, the fruit reveals itself and we experience the revelation.

Here, we are dealing with a true birth process, which we must set in motion and which we are all involved in. We thereby make a surprising discovery. Suddenly, we can do things that we could not do before. Suddenly, we no longer react with jealousy if our beloved is "unfaithful". Suddenly it is very easy to learn English. Or to take a header from great heights. Suddenly, everything is new, and one no longer has to spend a lot of time trying to learn things that one used to think of as being impossible. Even when dealing with serious illnesses, healing processes can be initiated in such a way that healing occurs instantaneously. I say this from experience. This experience occurs when the cycle for it is ripe.

Today, such a cycle is occurring all over the earth. We humans are living together with the earth in a beginning phase of unveiling – i.e. of revelation. This goes like a holo-wave through the entire earth, for the earth is a "holon". A holon is a concept from the field of holography. It is Greek and it means "the whole". In terms of biological and holographic systems theory, this whole has very special qualities that appear to us as pure miracles. We ought to get to know these miracle. How we deal with miracles is no longer a question of belief, it is a question of knowledge. If you are "in the cycle", you will experience the miracle of revelation, i.e. the old shells and crusts will fall off. They need to fall off both in the capitalist, money-oriented nations as well as for indigenous peoples. We need a concept of healing for the earth that applies to the West as well as to indigenous peoples and the oppressed farmers in Latin America.

Revelation initially means that the cruelty and violence in the world is revealed. Never have people died as massively and terribly as today, at this moment. But revelation also means that the new becomes visible at more and more places on earth – unveiling occurs. The unveiling makes it possible for us to take a look inside the nut. This innermost part is the "prehistoric utopia", that we deal with in our course of study.

This prehistoric utopia needs to be seen as clearly as possible by the project that is established. We need to train this kind of historic "seeing", which connects us with this "prehistoric utopia". The Sacred Matrix is prehistoric, it is beyond history, but it requires that we develop social and technical structures so that it can establish itself and "settle in" on earth, so to speak.

Revelation means that the world goes from the implicit to the explicit order. It changes from the latent state of its possibilities into the manifest state of its possibilities. A reality that so far existed as a latent reality, slowly manifests. The image of "prehistoric utopia" becomes visible.

We may ask ourselves if it is always the same image. What about objectivity? The answer is that the form of the image that is revealed is the one that corresponds to our times, to the beginning of the 21st century.

Every time has its own special image of "prehistoric utopia". If I look at the inside of the nut in May, I see a different "prehistoric utopia" than when I look at it in August. And yet it is always the same nut. In "prehistoric utopia", as in the nut, the Eternal connects with what I can currently manifest from the Eternal. The parable of the nut says everything about the connection between implicit and the explicit order, and between the Eternal and its manifestations, which always occurs historically, always cyclically.

Traditional society is the shell in which the nut was embedded until it became ripe. The ripe nut contains the seed for a new society, the Healing Biotopes and peace villages. These are so to speak the seeds of the coming world. All of a sudden the idea of Healing Biotopes can now catch on, for example in the Middle East, in Colombia, or Australia. We will see where it catches on.

For us it is a matter of finding which global vision is germinating and is pushing toward realisation today, at the beginning of the 21st century. Which vision wants to manifest? How should our gardens be designed? How do we build our houses, our living systems, our energy systems, our information systems? How do we regulate our social behaviour, our love relationships, the raising of our children? A new reality appears as the old crust is peeled away. A new image of a future human civilisation on earth is revealed. It is a new image of inhabiting our planet. It is the image of the Sacred Matrix. Whenever we build according to this image, real seeds of crystallisation of a new planetary field are created. When indigenous peoples join this field, they form a part of a new world community.

They, who up to now did not have any possibility to think ahead and to see a meaningful future for themselves, can now dream a joint dream together with us. This connection helps them gain power, new hope and a whole new image of their future.

If one is aware of the connection between image and manifestation, between "seeing" and "realising", then one knows of the importance that this dream has for real survival.

May a group be created in the Political Ashram in Tamera that is able to dream this image. We are thereby helping the world concretely and materially. It is by holding a new image of the future, with the help of new solar technology and new ecological methods of agriculture, that these people, the farmers of the so-called Third World and those belonging to indigenous tribes can participate in a global development that is increasingly becoming a main proponent for a new era. They, who up to now were oppressed, ignored or isolated, now belong to the "ruling party" in the global parliament.

This is not a question of going "back to nature" or "back to the ancestors", but forward to the realisation of the prehistoric utopia at the level of the 21st century.

A radical inner paradigm shift is required for us to be able to climb high enough on the energy ladder in order to see the global vision. "Seeing" is a question of energy. At a high level, science is a question of energy. In order to find this energy, a group in Tamera needs to place itself "under guidance" and state with fierce determination: "Not mine, but Thy will be done." For placing oneself "under guidance" means participating in the Sacred Matrix and its energy.

Chapter 8

A Virtual Space Station in the "Noosphere"

To introduce following chapter I want to say: It is a text written for those who are already familiar with the theory of global healing and who are working for a better future. But it is also relevant to others. It is a summary of different seminars on the relationship between vision and reality. I do not insist on definitions or terms, instead we need to gain an increasingly clear idea of the new centres, even before they can manifest materially.

The "space station" is a virtual Healing Biotope. It exists in the noosphere of our planet (the "noosphere" is the mental/spiritual world). In it we can see the development of a future life model for earth. We discover a different scenario than that prophecied by the future researchers of the 20th century. The scenario does not consist of the mechanics of a technology that has been infinitely extrapolated; instead, it is a concept for regulating our inner areas and for finding answers to the inner issues of life. The space station shows us a new life model, a "futuroscope" of the 21st century. And perhaps a new model for inhabiting the entire planet. If we look at the space station with our mental/spiritual telescope, we recognise facilities and forms of life that we cannot immediately realise on earth, but that can show us clearly in what direction the future lies. We gain a realistic vision. And we do not hesitate to realise it on earth.

The virtual space station is always developing, as an idea, ahead of the actual future centres on earth.

I speak of a "space station" for two reasons. First of all because it actually exists in the cosmic or mental area. Secondly, because it depends on we humans gaining an awareness of our place in the universe and of our consciousness of the relationship our terrestrial activities have with all other procedures of the cosmic world. In order to save our planet, cooperation with the whole universe is required. It is to be expected that an abrupt increase of power will occur through this cooperation, which brings the consciousness of the leading groups to new heights. Thanks to the sensors and cells, the super hologram of the brain and the "biological internet " of the DNA, we are well prepared for this cooperation. By learning to cooperate with the universe, we are afforded a type of assistance that we had forgotten existed.

The virtual system is located at the border between implicit and explicit order, between latent and manifested reality. It exists in real terms in the information space (space of consciousness) of the noosphere, without any indication of place and time. It is a virtual place, beyond the system of space and time, but with a clear tendency to manifest at different places on earth at the beginning of the 21st century. The term "virtual" implies the tendency to stimulate (still latent) conditions and systems to manifest themselves as soon as possible. One principle of the implementation consists of "seeing" the image that is to be materialised. We can call this "seeing" a "real vision", which to us appears much more objective than subjective fantasies. "Seeing the vision" is a substantial step for bringing latent possibilities into manifest reality.

The meaning of the word "virtual", as it is used here, lies somewhere between "latent" and "potential". The virtual system that is contained in a seed reveals and realises itself in the finished plant. In this sense, virtual systems possess a high power to manifest reality. All manifested realities have emerged from virtual systems (this may have been the initial thought in Plato's teachings about the "idea". It is also the initial thought in the mythology of the ancestors from the Aborigines and other indigenous peoples.)

The virtual space station is a virtual Healing Biotope. It is more objective, more comprehensive and it has been developed further than its counterpart on earth (in Tamera/Portugal), but it is always fed, examined, corrected and extended by it. Both systems are constantly in a relationship with each other and fertilise each other mutually. The virtual space station is of great importance for the implementation of the Healing Biotopes on earth. Beyond that, it has an important psychological effect. It "objectifies" the project so that it can be seen from a larger perspective and it thus keeps us from having too close a view of the respective reality on earth.

The project of the virtual station provides an important advantage for identifying our work "down here" and making it more professional. One sees the plan and knows what needs to be done. One is in the same situation as astronauts, who prepare for everything and know what needs to be done in every situation. They do not move arbitrarily; instead they follow clear guidelines. Their actions follow the laws of their spaceship. Translated to the co-workers of the Tamera project, this means that their actions follow the laws of the virtual Healing Biotope. They see the virtual entity and know what needs to be done.

Here, the term "virtual system" does not refer directly to computer simulations. Here, the term "virtual" means something like latent, possible, or prepared for manifestation. A virtual system that blazes the trail for our work contains a **development program**, which is focused on implementation. Some examples:

- DNA contains a virtual system that we can call the "dream" of life.
- A seed contains a virtual system. It is "the dream of the plant", as the Aborigines say.
- The core shape of human communities, called "prehistoric utopia" in the books by Sabine Lichtenfels, is a virtual system.
- Entelechy (inner target or potential form of all organisms) is a virtual system.

In this sense, a Healing Biotope or a planetary peace village is also a virtual system. As soon as its overall image has been perceived, it can be realised at many places on earth.

The theory of virtual systems and the development of virtual systems are main topics for research and teaching in the new university of Tamera. The idea of virtual systems is not new. We have been experiencing its technical implementation for some decades. When building a bridge that is difficult to construct, the virtual system for it is developed on a computer until it "functions". Today, a moving robot is placed on Mars, taking rock samples with a small probe and analysing them in a laboratory that is on board. Before being executed technically, the virtual system is "simulated" on a computer until it functions. This is a fantastic story that must be translated to the establishment of planetary Healing Biotopes, with new social, ecological and technological structures. (The professionals of virtual computer games do marvellous work here.)

The virtual space station is a virtual Healing Biotope that expresses universal life principles. It is a hologram of healing that is compressed as a latent reality until it increasingly materialises by going through a set of passages.

When we look at the virtual space station, we are looking at our own immanent possibilities. We thereby notice one special phenomenon: the inhabitants of the space station seem to be living totally free of stress in a kind of free, oscillating, effortless cooperation – and yet they are exceptionally efficient and have a great power of realisation. Gardens, installations, accommodations, information exchange systems and supply facilities that normally would take years to build are realised in an almost playful way. They seem to operate from a higher group consciousness, which gives each person his/her task and freedom, without any long discussions. It seems as if a kind of hyper consciousness has emerged in this entity, as is the case for ant colonies and beehives. The only difference is that here everything is done with full individual consciousness. Here, the principle of CIS (coherent information system), which we discussed during our last winter seminar in

Tamera, has become visible in an organic and vibrating way. It is not realised through drills and by force, not through group pressure and domination, but through – and this is the great word in the master plan of Creation – through self-organisation.

Now that we have gotten to know the incredible effect of "fields" through our own developments in the community, we recognise the existence of a real, immediately imminent, new communitarian consciousness. Taking this further, we recognise the existence of a global and universal consciousness network between all elements of consciousness in the world. We are connected with the coming world by a powerful bond.

The establishment of virtual systems takes place through the power of thought and information and through the creation of vision - always accompanied by conscientious material work, research and implementation. This applies to the Mars probe as well as to the centres of the future. It is dependent on the correct thoughts and information and on their continuous implementation in material practice. The necessary thoughts and "input" are not found through effort and material power, but by the activation of certain parts of the brain and certain frequencies of consciousness. This includes those practices of meditation that connect us with the "One Being", with what is the same in all entities. From the correct frequency of consciousness, the virtual system can be seen and perfected by the input of new information.

The "blueprint" for our coming reality has been developed. We can, to a certain extent, watch the virtual process, study it and understand more precisely, step by step, thought for thought and information for information, the nature of the space station and the nature of the network formation. We observe via a mental channel, a mental "telescope". We see the virtual being as a kind of vision that becomes increasingly clear to us the longer we are able to stay in the necessary frequency of mental perception, repeating it again and again. With each "vision formation" we bring this virtual being one step closer towards implementation (manifestation). We can observe, between which humans and groups, between which regions of the earth, which populations and centres cooperation begins to occur, resulting in the new global network. We can see, how this cooperation interacts with the space station and how new aspects, new lines and new emphases emerge there. We recognise the inevitable universal and planetary character of the whole process - and we see how ever more of it is condensing and becoming concrete in our material Project of the Healing Biotopes.

One can enter into an intimate relationship with the images of the germination of the world that is being born; one can see the powerful connections that want to condense and materialise onto earth. It is a process that always takes place in evolution anyway – it is only we who today notice and direct it consciously. For we humans are "the eye of evolution", and what we create in the material world works as a catalyst of this world-wide process.

I believe that in the thought system of our time, the concept of a virtual centre could be of genuine assistance in understanding the Political Theory.

It is with pleasure that I would like to quote a passage by the visionary language artist Satprem regarding the new centres (from his book: On the Way to Supermanhood):

City of the Future

The only law of the City of the Future, its only government, is as follows: a clear vision that accords with total Harmony, and spontaneously translates the perceived truth into action. The fakers are automatically eliminated by the very pressure of the force of truth, driven out, like fish, by a sheer excess of oxygen.

And if one day these ten or fifty people could build a single little pyramid of truth, whose every stone has been laid with the right note, the right vibration, simple love, a clear gaze and a call by the future, the whole city would actually be built, because they would have built the being of the future within themselves.

And perhaps the whole earth would find itself changed by it, because there is only one body. The difficulty of the one is the difficulty of the world, and the resistance and darkness of the one are the resistance and darkness of the whole world. That insignificant little enterprise consisting of a tiny city under the stars may well be the real enterprise of the world, the symbol of its transmutation, the alchemy of its pain, the possibility for a new earth through the single transfiguration of one piece of earth and one small part of mankind.

The virtual space station is a dream, but it is a realistic one.

In January 2006 I held a morning attunement with the title "Dream of the World". The thoughts and images of the virtual systems are here referred to as a "dream". In a certain sense, we are today actually living in "dreamtime". Evolution occurs in dreamtime, where new forms, new patterns and new possibilities are prepared. As I mentioned above, this is not only a subjective process, but a course of development of evolution. According to Robert Lawlor and Marlon Morgan, it dreams its new dream like the ancestors of the Aborigines dreamed their dream. From the books of Sabine Lichtenfels ("Dream Stones" and "Temple of Love") we can conclude how real such dreams are meant to be. They are real processes in the biosphere as well as in the noosphere of our planet, and they are just as material as the development of a plant from its seed.

I would now like to quote a passage from this morning attunement (spoken in meditation):

We live in a nascent universe and contribute our part to it. We have many trillion cells in our body. Every one of them contains the dream of life. The total dream of life is located in the genetic code. The seed of a eucalyptus tree incorporates the dream of the large tree. Pre-historic utopia, as represented by the stone circle in Almendres, includes a dream of mankind. There is a dream that lies, works and blows through every human being, every animal, every plant and every landscape.

As Josef von Eichendorff wrote:

"A song sleeps in all beings,
it dreams in them on and on,
the whole world rises up to sing,
if you just find the magic word."

There is a dream of the world. There is a dream for each entity and each being. There is also a dream of human beings. There is a dream of the whole of mankind and there is a dream of each single human being.

All these dreams seem to resonate in one large world dream. The dream does not arise from us; it is larger. It is dreamed by a higher subject, a higher networked consciousness.
We are dreamed.

From all these dreams, a potential universe emerges, a virtual entity, which we can look at, if we succeed in adjusting the necessary "reference beam", the necessary mental focus.

In this sense, for the staff of the Healing Biotope, one task is to learn to see the dream, to become seeing (be able to see) and perceive that latent possibility that now wants to be implemented. To perceive the latent reality of Healing Biotopes and peace villages that want to be realised now. To perceive self-sufficient centres, decentralized utility systems, new cooperation with nature and in new global networks that want to manifest now. To perceive new sensual, erotic, ethical and mental ways of behaving (behaviour patterns), that want to be realised now. To perceive new possibilities for inhabiting our planet and the global vision that is "dreamed" by the earth today.

It is good to not be too fixated on the material implementation, but to see the "plan" above it. Efficient work is directed towards the plan. The plan relieves us of a false sense of arbitrariness. We do not worry about our short-term needs; instead we are focusing on being of higher service to the world. An objectivity has entered into our subjective confusion. As soon as the first Healing Biotopes on earth reach this level of objectivity, the efficiency of the work will escalate. Just as the astronauts on their mission follow the operational principles of their spaceship, we follow the operational principles of the Healing Biotopes and their universal, cosmic networking. The more humans worldwide are able to cooperate in this oscillation, the faster the new system grows, both here on earth and there in the universe.

The future is always present. Every cocoon contains the information for the butterfly.
Thank you and Amen.

Chapter 9

Peace with Nature and All Fellow Creatures

(Excerpt from the book: The Sacred Matrix)

*"As long as humans torment, torture, and kill animals,
we will have war. "*
Bernard Shaw

Sunday morning. Today, I am in the bathtub and I notice some tiny animals on the tiles of the wall. They are very thin and maybe 3 millimeters long and they have many legs. I decide to regard them as ants. Where do they come from? What do they eat? What are they doing on this wall? I become curious, for they are my fellow creatures in evolution, they are real living beings, and they are a part of the one existence, so they must be cosmically related to me in some way. I watch them on their Sunday walk on the vertical wall and I see how they disappear into a little hole. That is their apartment. They have actually built themselves an apartment in the plaster between the tiles. What occurred in them, as they did this? Where did they get the enthusiasm and the power to be able to do something like that? Normally one sees them as a pest and cleans them off.

Here, two worlds collide with each other, and one of them, the older one, has to give way. This may be fully in line with Darwin, but is it also right in a higher sense? Do we humans really have the right to destroy an element of life as if this were natural, just because it doesn't fit into our own system of life? Is the ants' system of life wrong – or is ours? Maybe our own system of life is not quite correctly adapted to the higher order of Creation? Is there a possibility for non-violent co-existence?

Just a few decades ago such thinking would have been characterized as absurd, but today it becomes increasingly relevant with every further consideration, and with every new experience. Maybe there is a possibility for a kind of co-existence that encompasses all living beings? We will see.

Chaos research has taught me one thing: things that collide on the existing level of order can harmonize at a higher level of order. If enmities arise within a certain system, they can transform into friendship at the level of a system of a higher order. The solution of many issues consists in finding a higher level order.

All over the world, the agrarian production of food is connected to chemical warfare that human beings are waging against "pests". These are innumerable small living beings, who inhabit every field and every garden, and naturally want to partake in the harvest. There are, for example, worms, caterpillars, snails, bugs, aphids, mice, moles, etc. Chemical warfare is not aligned with the Sacred Matrix, for here the human being is destroying other organs that belong to the whole just as we do. There is an alternative, which has proven itself effective in small model projects.

There are non-violent gardens on earth. They are described in the book "In Harmonie mit den Naturwesen" ("In Harmony with the Beings of Nature ") by Eike Braunroth. The principle is based on communication with the so-called pests, not on their destruction. The peace gardeners use neither pesticides nor any other methods of deterrent against the small creatures. Peace is established through an agreement between human beings and their fellow creatures.

Jürgen Paulick, for example, a student of Eike Braunroth and until his death a co-worker at Tamera, made the following agreement:

I have planted a bed of lettuce, it belongs to all of us; I will harvest twelve heads of lettuce and you can have three."

Sometimes he put down such agreements in writing on a piece of paper that he then placed in the garden. I can imagine a nice heading in a tabloid newspaper: "Alternative Gardener Writes Letter to

Pests". At first we may react similarly and shake our heads. The only thing is that it works.

We in Tamera have had contact with animals in a way that one would not have believed was possible if one had not experienced it. It is based on the fact that we all – animals and human beings – are parts of the one existence and of the one consciousness. The information must be unambiguous and consistent. It must come from an authentic spirit of peace, not from reluctant concessions. In the surroundings, too, there must be no signs of violence or destruction, also not in the form of so-called complicity products, for whose production animals had to be killed.

Do snails know the number three? Probably not, but neither do they have to know it. A computer also does not have to understand what one inputs, and yet it does the right thing, because it was programmed to do so by a higher authority. We have a similar situation with the snails and the other animals. If we formulate our request clearly enough, and if it makes sense, it will be taken up by the information pattern which controls the snails and will be transmitted to the snail as a behavioral impulse. The same is true for a spider that is building its web. Does the spider know how to construct a web? The meta-intelligence, which operates in the body of the spider through the spider's information grid, knows how, and in the circuitry of Creation, that is enough.

In the case of the peace garden, horticulture is a spiritual process of information and cooperation, from beginning to end. Everything is one existence and one continuum: the garden soil, the plants, the animals, the human being, and the world of the microbes are all parts of one life body. All subjects that participate in this life body are connected with each other through the right frequency in one information circuit.

Chapter 10

Solar Age in Technology and Love

(Exerpt from a lecture without notes at the Tamera Summer University 2005)

The architect Le Corbusier once said:
"You do not start a revolution by fighting the state, but by presenting the solution."
Since the founding of our project, we have been working at the solution. What does it consist of? I begin with an illustrative example:

I have a strip of paper. It has two surfaces, the front and the back sides. We can imagine that they are two roads. A man is walking on one of the roads. He is totally in love. And on the back side there is a woman who is also totally in love. They are both in love with each other, but unfortunately they are on a two-dimensional surface, i.e. the front and back sides. They can never come together. One can imagine how their love grows, how their longing grows and what dreams they have. They probably now want to build rockets or invent something to be able to get fulfilment. They do not stand a chance. He is on one side and she is on the other. They cannot meet. This is a parable about the situation that lovers on earth have been experiencing for the last 3 000 years.

What does the solution look like?
I glue the paper strip together so that it forms a loop. But that, too, does not provide a solution. A circle itself won't do it. One of the two is still walking on one side, for example the inner side, whereas the other is on the outer side. But suddenly one has the idea of twisting one end of the strip by 180 degrees and then gluing it together. This is the so-called Möbius loop. It has the form of an infinity loop. Now the two of them are walking on the same

road that they were walking on before, but they cannot avoid running into each other's arms. This cannot be avoided. This is a very deep parable, that one can look at from many levels before one realises what it means. The parable applies not only to love, but to the solution of all problems.

What is being said is: "Human being, your problem cannot be solved at the level where it "lies". This is true for love. We cannot solve the issue of love at the level of couple relationships. We need the community for this as well as certain spiritual knowledge. This is true for everything else, too. It is true for technology. We cannot solve the problem of energy technology at the level where it lies today. We need a higher level of order.

In the case of the paper strip, the higher level of order consists of getting from the two-dimensional surface to the three-dimensional space through a twist.

The higher level of order in love consists of integrating oneself into a functioning community and a functioning spiritual system. That is the precondition for the two lovers to meet. When they then do meet, they meet in a good way. There are natural laws in love, just as there are in technology or religion, and they can be trusted as much as one trusts the law of gravity. To be precise, they are equally true or not true, for all laws, also the new ones, only apply ceteris paribus, i.e. if the other conditions correspond to this law. In another three thousand years we will be a bit further along in evolution and we will experience new things.

There are further examples that show that the solution lies in a higher level of order. A simple example is the following task: you have 6 matches and you are supposed to make four equilateral triangles with them. Once one has the solution, it is so incredibly clear that one does not understand why one couldn't see it immediately. (One goes to the third dimension and builds a pyramid.)

Let us continue with the issue of how we deal with nature. At a low level of order, we are exploiting nature. We believe that we know its physical laws, and we use them to make energy, food, machines, etc. from nature. This process benefits humans for a certain period of time. It does not at all serve nature. This behavior lies at a low level of order. Whenever conflicts are solved to the benefit of one or the other of the conflicting partners, we remain in the structure of war. In the heart of the world, we are creating the dynamics of war. At a higher level of order, our relationship to nature has to change so that it benefits both humans and nature. This means cooperating with nature.

I would like to continue with the topic of energy, a central issue of our time. Humanity needs a new energy concept. This applies both to technical energy and to the emotional energy of love and hate. At the heart of technical energy we find, in an expanded sense, solar energy. At the heart of emotional energy we find the areas of love and sexuality. We only become aware of the scope of these topics when we realise what incredible sources of energy we are dealing with.

As an example, when we speak of solar energy, we need to think on a completely different scale. For example, calculations show that the energy that the earth receives through solar radiation exceeds our overall energy needs on earth by a factor of 15,000. These are incredible orders of magnitude.

When we speak of emotional energy, we are dealing with equivalent sources of energy. We must realise this, too. Today, the whole earth is overwhelmed, overcome, shaken to the last house by the emotional energy of a humanity that can no longer be controlled. Hatred and violence are emotional energies. We should not judge anyone, for we must understand everything from within ourselves. We must understand from within what is happening in the world. Our future and the beginning of a new era are connected to consciously redirecting these energies, using them in a new way.

If we succeed in permanently ending the fight for the technical sources of energy, we will experience a whole different economic order over the entire earth as well as a totally different political culture. If we also succeed in transforming the emotional energies of hatred and violence into energies of solidarity, friendship and cooperation, then a totally new human community will emerge on earth.

This is not just a fantasy. It is knowledge that can be accessed. It constitutes unambiguous insights that emerge once you arrive at this sobering point. We obviously belong to a species that has to go through numerous mistakes in order to come to this point, to the source of extreme sobriety.

If both these endeavours were to succeed, the technical one and the redirection of the emotional energies, then we have a new earth and a new heaven. Then, an ancient promise will be fulfilled.

The solution can only consist of developing a model of society in which we find positive and convincing answers to both the technical and the emotional energy issues.

There are now two companies that have been working for an equal number of years to develop such a model. They are Sunvention in Lörrach in Germany and Tamera in Colos in Portugal. I am not saying that they are the only two. But I believe that these two companies are working at it at a unique level of continuity. As part of a healing model for the earth, one of the companies, Sunvention, is developing an encompassing technological structure, whereas the other company, Tamera, is developing a social structure. Both structures have now reached a level of maturity that makes it possible to fit one smoothly into the other. We are grateful for this development. In order to solve the issue of energy, both aspects of the issue, the outer as well as the inner, must be included.

First of all we must build a society that no longer is dependent on vicarious satisfaction, on compensation for unfulfilled lives. It is then also not dependent on the consumption of energy to which this vicarious satisfaction is connected. That is only logical. For this, a solid solution must be found for the human basic needs for a sense of belonging, trust, security, truth, love, sexuality and community.

Second, in order to arrive at the next highest level of order of energy, we must switch from the age of fossil fuels to the age of solar energy and cosmic energy. We must switch from depletable to inexhaustible sources of energy. The same is true for our forms of thinking. We must switch from a private or regional form of thinking to a universal or global form of thinking. This leads to everything else.

There are not so many places left on earth where one can do this in peace and joy. If one succeeds in solving the energy issue at one place on earth, then, according to the principle of morphogenetic field creation, it will inevitably also be solved at other places on earth. We will find new forms of cooperation with the sun and with plants in which solar energies are stored through the process of photosynthesis. We will be thankful for what the plants are doing every day. We also give thanks to the divine Spirit that allows us to understand the process of photosynthesis and, whenever necessary, to duplicate it. God did not make us just so that we could worship what is. God gave us a mind to let us participate in Creation and to multiply and intensify whatever exists at other places. That is the answer that nature is waiting for in its cooperation with humans. If we practice this way of seeing, then we are something like the eye of evolution.

The Solarvillage that is planned to be built here in Tamera is a pilot model in this direction. It provides an impetus for a new habitation of the planet. We are carrying out global work by creating a new model. We have to imagine what it really means when we use simple and transferable methods that can be put to use immediately at many places on earth. It means that villages that have several hundred inhabitants can be supplied with water, food, energy, heat and electricity. In the course of the further development, we will recognise that not only is the energy source that we call the sun – and we really do not know what the sun is – inexhaustible, but so are the possibilities for its use. The model that has been developed by Jürgen Kleinwächter opens up new paths for the evolution of technology.

The same applies to the inner sources of energy. The possibilities for using our emotional energies are inexhaustible and so are the possibilities for the use of solar energy. We will notice that both are identical. We will find ever more solar possibilities for nutrition, drinking, living, horticulture, ecology, material production, architecture, hot water production, etc. For our source of energy is no longer limited. Slowly our imagination begins to keep up with what is happening. Currently, it is only our perceived possibilities for use that are limited. But we are constantly discovering further uses, both in the technical and the emotional areas. Everything becomes a field of research, a field of discovery, art, theatre, "free love", everything that goes in this direction where our emotional energies gain a new power and orientation. The same applies to technology in the Solarvillage.

Jürgen Kleinwächter once said:

It is not the source, but our imagination that is limited.

A further main emphasis lies on globalisation. This deals with the creation of a global force for peace. For this we need regional and local self-sufficient centres. This is a difficult part of the political concept of the Healing Biotopes, but it must be understood. Why does the globalisation of the force for peace require the establishment of local centres? Why can local events and actions change anything globally? I can only ask that these centres and these new universitites be established, in which these things can be dealt with. Insights from systems theory, which were discovered in biology, are now gaining political importance.

Now we need to create a self-sufficient energy model. This is the only way out of the forced cycle of the globalized supply systems of energy, food and water. There is no other way. Otherwise we will die of thirst, of hunger or cold, when the corporations shut off supplies. It is only through functioning self-sufficient models that the solution can be generalised.

The conversion or transformation occurs mainly in three areas: in the technical, the social and the spiritual areas. It is a conversion that is based on the true global riches of our planet and our own life. Once such pilot models have been established, a movement is initiated which no longer is characterised by scarcity. I assume that this movement corresponds to the desires of humanity. A new kind of globalisation emerges. Old types of hopeless efforts give way to celebration and deep gratitude.

Chapter 11

Tamera and the "Monte Cerro" Experiment

(The ""Monte Cerro" Experiment began in Tamera on May 1, 2006. The following chapter contains the "Project Declaration 1" which was sent at that time to interested people, the media, potential sponsors and political initiatives.)

An Initial Project Overview

The development of humankind seems to be entering into a dead-end street and this cannot be overcome by traditional means. The work of the United Nations, NGO's and innumerable peace projects is both important and indispensable. However, it cannot hide the fact that there are hardly any positive projects and goals on a global scale any more. Under the circumstances, a convincing perspective for non-violent cohabitation of our planet is no longer visible. In order to create more favourable preconditions, centres would have to emerge in which the non-violent cohabitation of the human being with all co-creatures can be thought through and developed in an exemplary manner. **The aim of the Project of Healing Biotopes is to concretely establish such centres.**

The project consists of the development of international and, as far as possible, autonomous communitarian organisms, in which the living conditions for a non-violent future are researched and applied practically. It is the result of many years of research work in Germany, Switzerland and Portugal, where various groups have worked on a concept that could respond to the world-wide globalisation of violence with new thoughts for a world-wide globalisation of peace. During this time, close contact has been established with groups in Colombia (Gloria Cuartas, the peace village San José de Apartadó), India (Maria Mangte, Vasamalli Kurtaz from the Toda tribe, Bunker Roy, Barefoot College in Tilonia), Croatia

(Balkan Sunflowers) and especially in Israel and Palestine (Neve Shalom/Wahat-al-Salam, Hope Flower School, Holy Land Trust, CCRR, etc.) as well as to GEN (Global Ecovillage Network).

The new centres are defined as "Healing Biotopes" or "Peace Villages". The first such centre has been in development for some years now in the future workshop Tamera in Portugal. The next is planned for Israel/Palestine. What is to be developed in these centres is a type of "Biosphere 2", but no longer as a closed eco-system as it exists in Arizona. Instead what is created is a new living system that connects, in a non-violent way, the areas of life of human beings with those of nature, and the sociosphere with the biosphere. This requires establishing the necessary inner (social, human and spiritual) preconditions within human communities.

Within the framework of this project, the "Monte Cerro" Experiment is to take place on the 134 hectare site of the Tamera Healing Biotope I, starting on May 1, 2006. "Monte Cerro" is the (preliminary) name of the experiment and it is the Portuguese name of the site where it will take place. The participants of the experiment will live together, work together, and think together for three years. They will research the possibilities for the non-violent cohabitation of human beings and the cohabitation of humans with nature. All questions of cohabitation, such as the social organisation, the roles of the genders, ecology, ethics, etc., will be addressed in a new way.

The project represents a global aspect in two regards:

First: The economy of globalisation has torn humanity from its anchor. Such anchors are or were the land off which and on which one lived, life in the tribe or the extended family, an organic community organism, a far-reaching autonomous economy, being embedded into nature and Creation, and being at home under the protection of a greater whole. This natural anchoring is reflected in an inner value system of truth, trust, sticking together, mutual support, hospitality, helping one's neighbour, and taking care of the natural environment. This natural value system has been torn apart by a historical process of uprooting.

The totality of the capitalist "colonisation" (Edward Goldsmith) and its economic system has caused billions of people to lose their inner and outer anchor, their basic human values, their home, their trust and their meaning in life. The outer ecological and military destruction, which is inevitably linked to capitalist colonisation, corresponds to an immeasurable misery on the inside. The increase in the "epidemic" of crime, drug addiction, alcoholism, violence, depression and psychosomatic diseases are also a part of this.

Within this context, one can understand the wars of our time and the rage of killing and destruction. It is obvious that humanity has to find new forms of life in order to be able to end the era of terror. This global view automatically makes it absolutely necessary to build new community organisms in which the inhabitants can rediscover their natural values and resources at a new level. Such community organisms are to be built as models within the Healing Biotopes. The idea is not to copy old systems, but to develop new ones.

Second: The "new world order" that is the goal of globalisation, includes the cashless exchange of goods, electronic identity badges, so-called "free trade zones" and the extermination of all domestic subsistence economies. This means that an increasing part of the earth's population (indigenous peoples, the poor, the unemployed, the landless, the sick, opposition groups, freedom fighters, truth seekers, autonomous thinkers and unpopular inventors) are excluded from the supply of goods. Moreover, since one result of unemployment is the decline of purchasing power, a part of the production becomes meaningless and unemployment, in turn, increases again. A special kind of global vacuum then emerges as the part of the earth's population that drops out of the economic system will need a new form of living. Here, too, the Healing Biotopes could present possibilities for solutions. The new community organisms that are to be established are independent of banks, multinational corporations or states and will have a mostly autonomous supply in all vital areas. In a sense, it is a "return" to local systems of economy that are based on community, but they are connected with new technologies and new social structures, including a new relation between the sexes.

How can local groups have a global effect? How can the conditions of structural peace that are created at a few places on earth have an effect on the whole earth?

The answer lies in the characteristics of holistic, all-encompassing systems. The functioning and parameters of such systems have been described in detail in the previous chapters of this book. Publisher's note.

What will determine the success of such peace projects is not how big and strong they are (compared to the existing apparatus of violence), but how comprehensive and complex they are, how many elements of life they combine and unite in a positive way. When establishing new fields in evolution, it is not the "law of the strongest", but the "success of the more comprehensive" that is determinant. Otherwise, no new developments could have been able to establish themselves, for when they began, they were all "small and inconspicuous" (Teilhard de Chardin).

In this context we can formulate the central research question of the Healing Biotopes as follows: which social, ecological, economic and spiritual preconditions must be realised so that – on the basis of the current state of our evolution – the general information necessary for planetary healing work can emerge?

The main problem is not the question of whether the centres can be globally effective but whether we are able to really create them. Since they are a part of the whole, the burden of the whole also rests on them. They can only be successful if they reach the "universal foundation" that they share with the whole. That universal foundation is the indestructible basis for all human beings, it is their common source and inheritance, their divine core. It shows itself in the capacity for truth and love and in the acceptance of the higher orders of life. Communities begin to be globally effective once they have found, in the tapestry of humankind, the very dimension in which all inhabitants of the earth are connected to one another. It is on this basis that the fragments of life, which have been separate for so long, converge and unite: man with woman, human being with human being, sexuality with the mind/spirit, Eros with Agape, human being with nature, human being with God. Here, the indispensable spiritual dimension of future healing work becomes apparent. Healing is the return from being banished, it is the negation of the original pain that consisted of separation.

The "Monte Cerro" Experiment

We begin with a thought experiment. Imagine the Spirit of the World coming to a group of people and giving them the following task:

"You are to find out under what circumstances the earth can be healed. For this, you have your mind and your spirit, your body, your ability to communicate and the entire knowledge that humans have gathered at your disposal. First, you must find out how you yourselves can live together in a non-violent, healing way among yourselves and with the creatures of nature. Start all over again, and use all your intelligence, your knowledge and abilities, your collective power, intuition and vision in order to find a common way.

The suffering of the world, including your own, has been caused by human beings and thus it can also be healed by human beings if they find out how. I will give you three years for this research project. The essential elements of the healing process should have been found by then. Open your minds/spirits to my presence, for I will help you when you need help. I wish you much courage and joy of discovery in your work."

We are, in fact, planning to turn this story into reality. Many people who feel the apocalyptic pressure of our times are now ready to cooperate fully with all they can in a project of this size. Since the experiment has been in preparation for more than 25 years, we will not begin with a "tabula rasa". During these 25 years, a group of experienced work group leaders has emerged, consisting of Sabine Lichtenfels (theologian, co-founder of the overall project), Rainer Ehrenpreis (physicist), Paul Gisler (automobile mechanic), Roland Luder (physicist), Oskar Eckmann (teacher), Amelie Weimar (medical doctor), Barbara Kovats and others.

For several years Tamera has also been operating a school of peace, in which especially young people have been prepared for the tasks and professions of future peace work. The training takes three years. The "Monte Cerro" Experiment itself constitutes a phase of such a training. The training incorporates theoretical lessons, training in craftsmanship, historic expeditions and deployment to areas of crisis. Through their experiences on location (in Israel, Palestine, Croatia, Bosnia, Colombia and India), the future peace workers will get to know the thoughts and goals of the global peace work. Those who have seen with their own eyes, felt with their own bodies and understood with their own heart what is occurring today all over the world, will participate in a deeper way in the establishment of a humane alternative. The world needs help!

The model character of the experiment requires a mostly autonomous supply of food, drinking water and energy. Since the future Healing Biotopes must free themselves from any dependency on the supply and economic systems in society, the demand that they be autonomous in this sense is not only an ecological requirement, but also an ethical one. We must also know where the food that we eat comes from. Gradually, this will also apply to other areas of consumption. The experiment at "Monte Cerro" has 134 hectares of poor soil at its disposal, which can be turned into a fertile biotope. From our experience with permaculture (Holzer, Fukuoka etc.), with communication with plants (Findhorn,

Dorothy McLean), with peace gardens (Eike Braunroth), with aqua culture and water healing (Schauberger and others), with solar technology (Kleinwächter and others), with energy work and geomantics (Pogacnik and others), new ecological concepts have emerged that have a significance that surpasses the local conditions. The soil and vegetation of the whole region urgently needs a comprehensive biological and geomantic healing.

A New Relationship to Nature

For our conduct with nature, we apply the following principle, which was formulated by Albert Schweitzer:

Reverence towards life and respect towards all fellow creatures.

This includes creating a living system that fits in to nature and also gives the animals space when they seek contact with human beings. This not only applies to what is already accepted as domestic animals, but also for animals such as mice, rats, birds or toads. They have an important place in Creation.

The aim of the Healing Biotopes includes changing our behaviour toward the living beings of nature in general and also a non-violent approach to so-called vermin. They are all part of the big family we call life. Nature beings ("Devas") follow a mental/spiritual orientation that is designed for cooperation with the human being. Human beings and animals form a planetary community. In the Sacred Matrix of Creation, they are not destined for war but for co-evolution and cooperation. We are not only working for our own survival; we are also working for a model of a non-violent, sustainable ecology in harmony with the laws of life of the biosphere.

Basic Research: Structures of Reality

Parallel with the practical projects, there will be a department for basic research in the (planned) university. It will deal with energy research (possibilities to use "free", cosmic energy etc.), matter research (what is matter actually?), water research and flow research (Alfred Wakeman, Theodor Schwenk and Victor

Schauberger) and oscillation and resonance research. It will also be engaged in life research, research on the functional and structural logic of living matter, on the principle of power, the effectiveness of field forces, the phenomena of "synchronicity" of mental/spiritual and material events and the principle of spiritual attraction. It will also deal with non-material cycles of subtle energies and information, harmonics research, the effect of sound on the processes of life, the significance of the egg shape, etc.

Basic research is directed toward technological and ecological renewal, but it will increasingly connect with consciousness research, since there are ultimately mental/spiritual forces that control the material world. The basis for the structure of reality is a mental/ spiritual matrix. Therefore, healing work that aims to change our material environment is always also work on the mental/spiritual matrix. (This includes research into the mental/spiritual areas of "prayer research", meditation, ethics, vision work etc.)

Art

The cultural life of the project is comprised of all forms of artistic work: painting, music, dancing, theatre, placing stones and sculptures in the landscape for healing, landscape design and various other work.

Among other things, this deals with rediscovering design principles that are used by Creation itself, such as unintentional actions that have a high accuracy and success rate, effortless concentration and dealing with difficulties in a playful way (Wu-Wei and Mo-Chi-Chu in Taoism). In this sense, art is the conscious application of autonomous processes of Creation, thus approaching the original context of art and cult. Joy and creative energies are produced through communitarian actions and humorous rituals. Artistic actions, as documented for example in our art brochure "Die Wäscheleine" (The Clothesline) are a part of the healing process of a coming culture. The establishment of an arts hall as an art gallery and theatre space, an open air studio and a special building ("futuroscope") for the performance of futurist theatre pieces are all planned.

Further Areas of Work

Below, I will mention some important work areas, for which further co-workers and specialists are needed.

Workshop, crafts and technology – establishing a place for youth – the youth school – raising children – the guest area – the horse project – handicrafts – the shop – healing – political and human networking – the media agency – the computer network – congresses and events – the kitchen, nutrition etc. - administration – the economy - ecology ...

In the long run, all this can only succeed on the basis of a stable community that functions in the human area. That takes us to the issue of community, one of the core issues of the project that cannot be outlined in a few sentences. We cannot put the best goals into practise unless we are able to establish functioning communities that have the ability to survive. Ecological humanism requires a new social structure. Throughout the history of the project, surprising experiences have been gathered in the area of human cohabitation, and they have made us think more deeply about community building and solidarity.

Some Questions regarding the Experiment

The participants are supposed to learn how to live and work together harmoniously. Also, they will cooperate in the work on the historical issues of humankind of our time and find a path of healing. It is a small model society, where the basic questions have to be asked again, without relying on pre-fabricated answers:

How much leadership does a community of this size need?
· How can efficient coordination of the various working areas be guaranteed?
· What is the healthy relation of individual free space and the need of the community?
· What forms of life and work awakens the highest potential in the individual?
· What makes a human being permanently happy?

- How can conflicts be solved?
- How can the difficulties in the relationship between the sexes be solved?
- How can our fellow creatures in nature be involved in the peace work?
- How can we live together with animals that nest in our houses and gardens because they seek to be close to human beings (birds, mice, rats, toads, snakes and other so-called "vermin")?
- How can one communicate with nature beings (Devas)?
- What do educational programmes look like that make sense to young people?
- How can the healthy development of children be promoted?
- What is healthy nutrition?
- How can spring water and drinking water be revitalised?
- How can communitarian consumption be limited to those essential products which do not contribute to global exploitation - we call them "complicity-free" products - without returning to the level of cave people?
- How can we develop recycling systems with a maximum use of the waste? ("Nature doesn't know waste.")
- How is it possible to work in a concentrated way for a long time without getting tired?
- What does a spiritual life look like in practise when it comes from personal experience?
- How can a lively network be organised?
- How can a common vibration of calm and joy be created in the face of the abundance of tasks?

We assume that not all of these questions will find ready answers, for we find ourselves in a universe in process. We believe, however, that if we do a good job, the directions in which we can find convincing solutions will become clearer and crystallise. We are dealing with finding a new way for cohabitation in the human biotope, a way where the human order can reconnect with the order of life and Creation.

The Spiritual Anchor

All earthly life is woven into cosmic life, and there is no basic separation between this world and the next world, between earthly and cosmic, between the material and the mental/spiritual world. The tasks that must be completed could not be solved if divine help were not to come to our aid from the whole of the world. On the one hand, the (entelechial) forces of self-healing, which are inherent in all areas of life, must simply be stimulated in the right way to reach their goal. On the other hand, there are spontaneously operating "field forces" that always become active when new developments are in resonance with the whole. A basic aim of our project is to enter into lasting cooperation with the Sacred Matrix. It is the power of Creation, the basic pattern of the "implicit order" (David Bohm), that is the basis of all things and all life forms and regulates their relations.

The spiritual focus of the project is not directed towards the next life but towards the physical, sensual world on earth. The participants will therefore rediscover the female sources that were suppressed for thousands of years, and will integrate them into their future work. (This explains the high significance of the issues of love, sexuality and new roles for the sexes.)

At the moment, a special "Ashram" is in development, a place where cooperation with the forces of Creation can be learned. All project participants have the possibility to practise their spiritual exercises or to go on retreats in this space. The establishment of functioning future communities will no longer be possible without the establishment of solid spiritual foundations. A new culture emerges from the reconnection with the divine laws of life and the universe. There are certainly many paths to this goal, but there is maybe only one key to open the gateway: the rediscovered quality of **TRUST**.

Preconditions for Participation

We are often asked what preconditions for cooperation and participation people must fulfill to be able to participate in the experiment. What matters is one's inner willingness to cooperate and the extent to which one's human qualities conform to what we consider to be the "ethical basis" for the project:

· truth
· mutual support
· assuming responsibility for the community.

These are no minor qualities. They do not depend on the individual's academic degree or professional position, but only on his or her state of consciousness. We must apply the measures that the world needs for its healing to ourselves, too. Participants must, therefore, be ready to open up to a high degree of self-change and to overcome old habits.

"Monte Cerro" itself is mainly intended for young people between the ages of 18 and 40, who are willing to take on the tasks and professions that are necessary for establishing Healing Biotopes. Older people are also warmly welcome, if they can adjust to the new life circumstances. Participants know that crises and conflicts are unavoidable in such a novel experiment. They are committed to seeing the coming difficulties as a part of their path of learning and – if at all possible – to stay for the entire three years. It is therefore important that they inform themselves thoroughly about the meaning and the purpose of this experiment beforehand. People with leadership abilities and team spirit, experts in the areas of ecology, technology (energy, water, information), architecture, administration and medicine, are particularly wanted.

Community as a Research Issue

It will only be possible to carry out the tasks listed above on the basis of a well functioning community. Ever since the sixties, so many community projects have failed due to unsolved human conflicts so we must not be naive in this area. If we want to put into practise a sustainable form of ecological humanism, we must find a form of humane, social and sexual humanism that liberates the participants from the burdens and pains of the past. The difficulties that stand in the way of a world-wide healing process, lie not only in the outside world but also in ourselves. Above all, the fields of conflict about money, power, love and sex form inner barriers that cannot be overcome by mere appeals for peace. In our daily life together, it is very simple things, such as an unfulfilled need for contact, a striving for dominance, competition for love and sex, jealousy, unconscious negative projections, the fear of being judged etc., that have destroyed groups from the inside in hundreds of projects since the sixties. Since these factors are not only individual defects, but mainly the consequences of a collective cultural disease, they can not then be permanently resolved at an individual level.

We all carry the original pain of a great wound inside us. We have all received many wounds in the course of our karmic life journeys. Healing work, as we mean it here, means healing these wounds in oneself and others. This is the task and this is also the promise that was given to us through the divine parable in the previous chapter: you can and you shall heal the old wounds. The signposts for this are truth, mutual support, responsibility for the community and service to life. Also, help others so that you will be helped, too.

Here, we come to a deeper definition of "sustainability". The necessary ecological changes require human change and it can only happen in a lasting way if we go to the roots and develop new basic patterns for culture and society. Establishing trust among people and making transparency possible between people is not only an individual but mainly a societal, cultural and political issue. This is a basic thought of the Project of the Healing Biotopes. We must develop communities in which lies, deceit and betrayal no longer provide an evolutionary advantage. We need new societal structures that make a durable cohabitation in truth, love and trust possible. It is a difficult historical heritage that is besieging our individual existences in the most intimate of spaces. This issue must be solved in such a way that the healing forces of entelechy can be fully liberated and can take full effect.

The research of the Project of the Healing Biotopes deals with the development of future communities that can offer their participants new experiences of healing and development that come from a new experience of trust. Such communities inevitably go through a series of inner experiments, with which they extend their present borders and gain new terrain. It is about pushing borders outward, making it possible for new inner focal points to emerge in one's own life. It is a research adventure of great significance, perhaps the biggest adventure of our time.

One might wonder and ask whether it is necessary to invest so much work and time in intense research work in order to establish functioning communities and develop new life forms that are stable and sustainable. The answer is unambiguous: yes, it is necessary. Up to now, the alternative models of simple life have never worked for any long period of time, because they were not able to counter the immanent destructive forces of modern times. The problems that need to be solved at the end of a patriarchal, capitalist-imperialist era can no longer be solved at the level of ancient Christian or Buddhist agrarian communism (even if this could temporarily help many participants). The issues of our time are so closely networked and so closely linked to each other that they cannot be solved individually. A truly non-violent ecology cannot be developed without a new relation to our own inner nature, for outer nature and inner nature are two sides of the same issue and they are moved by the same life energies. As long as we suppress our own nature and deny it, we will hardly have a loving relation with our co-creatures in outer nature. The same is true for technology and medicine. The paradigm shift that is needed requires increasing cooperation with those inner forces that have so far mostly been suppressed and fought against. These mental/spiritual forces operate in all living matter. Teilhard de Chardin described them as the "inside" of things, thereby opening up a new view of the material world. The cosmic, super-conscious, subconscious or suppressed forces that so far have been attributed to the separate areas of deep psychology, religion, magic and art, must gradually be integrated into a conscious way of living, so that we can dissolve the latent schizophrenia of our contemporary culture. This means creating a new image of ourselves as human beings.

The most powerful guarantor for the success of the work is the field-building forces that begin to operate in every community as soon as agreement is found among the participants regarding new experiences and overcoming boundaries. It is then no longer only one's own force, but mainly the force of the field that enables the participants to have new experiences. Then, we must no longer do everything ourselves. We do what we can and the rest, we "let God do."

Some psychological criteria of modern high tech work should be applied to the interpersonal, spiritual and ecological research work in such a way that an efficient and permanent power of peace can emerge. These criteria have to do with spiritual/mental energy, will power, continuity and looking forward to the results with joy. They include believing in success, being willing to go beyond almost any limitation, and declaring that what so far seemed to be impossible is in fact possible. Here, experimentation and research is called for, not clinging to old beliefs. In the stormy processes of transformation of our times, the universe, which is in a constant state of becoming, constantly projects new futures onto the horizon of our vision circle. Research work in the inter-personal and the communitarian areas always also entails keeping up with these developments without stress. The appropriate calm is dependent on finding the right speed. The proper attitude is provided by our will, which prepares us for a long and difficult process. Here, it becomes apparent that our mental and physical condition is very important.

One can imagine the dimension of the issues that a group of people will have to deal with if it wants to take on the task that it was given by the Spirit of the World in the parable above. But does not the basic rule also apply here, that the greater the tasks are, the greater the power that comes to our aid?

The Big Topic of Sexuality, Love and Partnership

Give us mercy and redeem us.
We, too, were searching for love –
for the coming together of man and woman.
(Words that were received in a dream from the dreamer's deceased father.)

The love between man and woman is one of the most beautiful things that one can experience on our earth. Nobody who is in this state of love can imagine that it will ever be over. All the same, almost all love relations fail. Human society has a collective heartache. For most people, the area in which they could have the most beautiful experiences is an area of deep disappointment, deep suffering, deep anger and often ultimate resignation.

The issue of love is a global issue. "There cannot be peace in the world as long as there is war in love." What is meant here is the daily "little war" between the sexes – with its bad consequences for the children. These are children who will later go into war as soldiers and devastate the earth. These children were born to parents who for the most part were unable to show a convincing model of love. From generation to generation, the earth finds itself in a situation of unfulfilled love, leading to ever worsening pain and devastation. The inner context between unfulfilled love on the one hand and disease or merciless brutality on the other can today be seen in every orphanage and in every biography of violent youngsters. We find it in the life story of all dictators (see the works of Alice Miller), and we also find it in psychosomatic diseases if we know how to interpret the symptoms correctly. "All you need is love." Humankind needs fulfilment in love in order to resurrect.

What kind of love is meant here?

Every love. Sensual love, soul love, religious love, loving your neighbour, loving animals, partner love. The focus lies in the reconnection of the two halves of the human being: man and woman. At the core of human cohabitation is the cohabitation between the genders. Their attraction or repulsion, their sexual signals and their interactions, and their hopes and disappointments run like a secret nervous system through the whole of human society, through every office, every department store, every meeting, and every group. The two halves of the human being long for each other, yet they fail to meet each other, they fight each other and search for each other until they find each other. **They must find each other, not only two of them, but world-wide, for only then can the deepest of all wounds be healed.**

The happiness or misery of children – and thus of all people, for we were all once children - depends above all on a harmonious connection between man and woman. After thousands of years of suppression and denial during the patriarchal era, the healing of love between the genders is probably the most revolutionary step in the current healing work. A new, humane culture is rooted in a new relation between the genders.

We are, therefore facing the central research question: how can the (open or latent) war between the genders be ended efficiently and be replaced by permanent and reliable solidarity? How can the happiness of two people in love be protected and maintained permanently, without them having to protect it with fences that are too high? Is there a realistic model of love, in which the wishes for partnership are compatible with the wishes for sexual adventure, and where the longing for faithfulness and intimacy is not connected with the fear of loss and clinging to one other? Is there a form of living together, in which the sexual affection of one human being to another no longer provokes fear, anger and revenge in a third person? Into what kind of human culture, what structure of trust, and what form of interpersonal human truth and acceptance can such a love be embedded? At what level of higher order are partnership, love and free sexuality compatible with one another? Under what social, sexual, ethical, and spiritual conditions is a lasting fulfilled love possible? Is there a relation between religion and Eros that enhances and unites both sides?

We cannot provide ideological answers to these questions.

Instead, we are looking for new spaces of experience, for truth and insight. The new era needs a new image of love and new role models for man and woman. This issue is the core issue of the planetary transformation process with which we are faced. It can only be solved together with all other subjects. **The solution does not begin by taking a stand for monogamy, polygamy or celibacy, but by taking a stand for an inner truth that is supported by the truth of others. Healing comes from a field of truth.** The inner truth that comes from the source can manifest itself both as temporary celibacy and as the physical pleasure of polygamy, depending on the state of development that the individual is going through. All variants will probably be experienced on the path toward truth, until we reach a common understanding and enlightenment here – in the most difficult and most secret of areas. From then on, a burden will be lifted from the heart of humanity.

Healing Processes in the Community through the Establishment of Trust

"Happiness is being at home in something greater."

The fulfilment of life also depends on how I answer the question: for whom or what are you doing all this? If the answer is convincingly directed towards something greater than one's own person, a fulfilled life could be in sight. Personal problems require a higher level of order in order to be solved. Such a higher level of order is community. Community means living on a communitarian instead of a private basis. The mental and moral shift from a private to a communitarian way of life may be one of the most radical paradigm shifts. It is only in this way that we can permanently dismantle the mechanisms of protection and defence with which the isolated human beings of our time have had to familiarise themselves. The Project of the Healing Biotopes has suffered some massive strokes of fate in its 25 years history. How could the com-

110

munity survive them? It survived because it had developed a stable energy field that held the participants together. The participants were already sufficiently familiar with the rules of a communitarian way of life to not fall into individual resignation.

Community means to really get to know other people and see who they really are. We gradually enter the human world that lies beyond the facade of fiction. Here, we find real encounters from centre to centre and from truth to truth, and the result is genuine trust. Trust is the most original and most efficient of all healing forces. The very first task of a community is therefore to create trust among the participants. Can you sense what this means? Do we know how many wedges were driven between human beings during the patriarchal era: between man and woman, parents and children, young and old, peoples and cultures. The task of re-establishing lost original trust is equivalent with the task of activating completely new chains of information in the genetic code of humanity. Old patterns of conduct must be abandoned and replaced by new ones. It is a learning process beyond comparison. But isn't Elisabeth Kübler-Ross right when she says that all learning processes in life in the end result in having to learn to love? And should we not be able to do that? Let us look from a greater distance to this question. Humanity has built stations in space, invented self-guiding missiles, de-ciphered the genetic code and shot at cancer cells with nano-cannons – should it not be able to solve its inner problems with the same effort and the same persistence?

Chapter 12

GRACE – A Pilgrimage for Peace

Together with Benjamin von Mendelssohn, the head of the Middle East Initiative at Tamera, Sabine Lichtenfels, the co-founder of Tamera, headed up a group of pilgrims through Israel and Palestine in November 2005. The peace action was called "GRACE". In advance of this pilgrimage, she wrote a preparatory text:

Those who are against war need a livable vision for peace. The globalisation of violence can only be overcome through a realistic globalisation of peace. This year I am placing my work under the motto of doing everything I can to find and spread the frequency of peace. I will use all my power to end the inner and outer war on earth.

We have chosen the Middle East because here we find one of the great acupuncture points, which determine if we will have war or peace on earth. According to our plan, an international peace village is to be built there as soon as possible. The peace march is to end with a larger final rally in Jerusalem.

Let the soldiers become human beings again! They have fought enough. Let us organise a large peace camp together with them, where they can learn love and not war. I appeal to well-known musicians and artists: give this project your voice. Help us to develop a new perspective in the Middle East and help us make the voice of peace heard all over the world.

Sabine Lichtenfels began her pilgrimage in June 2005 in Southern Germany. Mostly, she travelled alone, without money and on foot. She was often invited to speak about the meaning and purpose of her action. At the end of October she was in Israel, where approx. 40 people had gathered to participate in the risky pilgrimage through the West Bank to Bethlehem and Jerusalem. Together with the theatre group from Tamera, she put on a self-produced theatre piece called "We refuse to be enemies". On November 9th, she held a peace event at the wall in Israel near the Arab village of Baqqa al Garbye together with her group of pilgrims. On the same day, in solidarity and connection to her action, peace events were held in many places around the world, one of them also in Auschwitz.

The night of the 9th to the 10th of November in 1938 is the Night of the Pogrom of the Third Reich, in belittling terms also called the "Night of Broken Glass", when the first big hit of the Nazis against the Jews was carried out in Hitler's Germany.

It is also the day of the opening of the Berlin Wall in 1989.

On this day of remembrance, the "GRACE" group of pilgrims held a night vigil in front of the wall near Baqqa al Garbye. They had organised a projector, with which they could project images and texts onto the wall. In the morning Sabine Lichtenfels held a speech, a "wall meditation". Here are some excerpts from this speech:

See on one side the Palestinian people with their pain, their longing for freedom and their cultural origins.

See on the other side the people of Israel with their culture, their wounds and their centuries-old longing for protection and a feeling of home.

Imagine representatives from both peoples, accompanied by friends from all over the world, slowly approaching the wall with the intent of overcoming the wall of separation. Mothers from both sides reach out their hands with the firm determination to no longer let their children become victims of violence and war.

Imagine that there, where the wall was originally, Israeli and Palestinian farmers now plant gardens – with olive trees as a symbol of a long-lasting peace. The wounds of fascism start to heal, for the souls of the perpetrators at the time – both the dead and the living – recognise their deep aberration and their guilt. They sincerely ask forgiveness of their victims.

Imagine that the seed for future cultures of peace are placed in your hand – a cosmogram, a letter in the alphabet of life for the process of

113

reconciliation. Imagine that you are now planting this seed in the earth here at this wall. Imagine that the seed sprouts and begins to bloom at different places on earth.

Light your light and make yourself into a power that will not rest until peace on earth has been realised.

Imagine that cheering people on both sides greet the dismantling of the wall. They now see each other as friends. Their difference no longer awakens enmity, but interest.

May we all find our own way of designing the one and only source of life and love. May we all, in our own way, rediscover and celebrate the sacred core of life.

In this sense, we light the light for peace in the Promised Land, for peace on earth, and for peace between all beings.

Blessed be this process."

In her book "GRACE", Sabine Lichtenfels writes:

When I am travelling in the name of "GRACE", I first try to meet people and let myself be touched by them and not by the world view that they represent. Whenever our meetings began with debates about world views, everything was lost. Nobody listened any more and instead the emotional chaos immediately started to kick in. The meetings occurred totally differently if human contact had been made and we had touched each other first.

Once, when I saw a young Israeli officer, who was full of conviction and was explaining the ideological values of his state, I wanted to cry out in anger and outrage. Then I suddenly realised that he could have been my son. Immediately, I saw the human being in him.

That is the first step that creates an opening. Now, it becomes a question of if I am able to tell him the truth that I see with no fear. In the state of "GRACE" I do not judge, but I have the courage to speak the truth. I want to speak the truth so that it reaches the other person and changes him or her in such a way that it does not intensify the war. "GRACE" reminds us that behind this terrible dimension, which soon does not seem to provide any way out, a different truth and a different reality reign. It is a very simple truth. It applies not only to the Middle

East, for it is the same everywhere. The truth differs from ideologies by being plain and simple. It was distressing for me to see that in most cases the conflicts kept getting new fuel through the world views and convictions with which everyone hit each other on the head.

You see it in more or less bad forms, but the basic pattern is the same everywhere. It reveals itself behind all ideologies, all religions and all world views. We have all equally become victims of the imperialist culture.

Behind this rolling avalanche, which flows like a wave over the areas of crisis of this earth and records the experiences of pain in the history of victims and perpetrators, behind all this you will find the same hunger. It is the hunger for life, the hunger for love, the hunger for trust and the feeling of belonging and the hunger for acceptance and recognition. It is the hunger for being seen and understood. This hunger is independent of any culture. It is simply there, in every person, as sure as he or she has remained human.

"GRACE" is like a consciously chosen naivety, which helps you not to get lost in the ocean of world views, but to see and protect the elementary and simple truth in everything. You create openings for the cry for life. You see the collective pain body of the Jews before you, which is connected to their terrible fate during the last two thousand years. You see the collective delusion of the Germans in the fact that up to today they have not been able to really understand and heal their past. You see the consequences of a partriarchal religion and culture that have gone off on a wrong track, producing wars for thousands of years that are like nature´s spectacle of fantastic thunderstorms.

The whole story of victims and perpetrators must end. Here, world history is waiting for the great transformation, the great awakening.

"GRACE" reminds us of the sacredness of life at every moment. "GRACE" reminds us that there can only be a way out if, as humanity, we succeed in returning to the true foundations of life and love, of trust and truth.

On the topic of guilt, she writes:

This system of guilt is based on one party being right and the other wrong. This kind of thinking leads you to the conviction that it is permitted to wage war against evil. Some people have to make very painful experiences as perpetrators or victims in order to see through this mechanism themselves and finally abandon it. For under this system, peace can never come about.

One's own guilt is suppressed by placing the blame on someone else. This mechanism operates especially collectively and can therefore so easily be disguised. When many people are of the same opinion, one can easily be convinced that it is the truth. Who has the ability to keep their own inner light of longing and insight alive and to keep on asking questions, shining their light into the dark areas that everybody is avoiding?

Here, common sense states that it can become lonely and also dangerous, and already you are willing to follow a collective habit and adopt the opinion that everybody thinks is correct. Add to this our great longing to belong to a group. One does not want to be an outsider and to go against the opinion of all one's friends. So, one conforms.

If someone now comes and tries to make you aware of the real truth and thus touches your inner wound, then everything in you starts resisting. You immediately go on the offensive, for otherwise your whole system could break down and a truth that you are very afraid of could come to light.

In this system someone always has to be to blame, and fundamentally, the others are to blame. That is the mechanism that works wonderfully, it ensures the cohesion of the group and it keeps war alive. Entire empires can be held together through this mechanism. Who is forcing us to identify with a system and a story that again and again has led to the same acts of cruelty, war, torture, mutilation, and physical and emotional illness?

During our pilgrimage we often meet people who have stepped out of the old system of guilt and have already decided to follow a whole different ethic. The suffering often has to be very deep, in order for a person to be able to make this decision.

Michal, whom we met close to the Holocaust Museum, not far from Jerusalem in the Jerusalem Forest, was an example of this. Years ago, we met her at this very place, and we had noticed her because of her youth, her beauty and purity. Three years ago she became the victim of a suicide bombing in a bus and it was a miracle that she survived. She now sat in our tent, telling us about her experiences. She was in a coma for two months and the doctors had given up on her. She was so disfigured that even her parents could not recognise her. During the course of the years, she has regained her beauty, even if it is marked by scars. She keeps emphasising that she never reacted with anger against the perpetrators. She said: „If I had been in their situation, I might have done the same thing. To me it is only important that you see that there are always two sides to everything." She is speaking with difficulty as she says: "I was 23 years old, but my body was like that of a baby. I had to learn everything anew - eating, speaking, going to the bathroom. I had nightmares every night. And yet I do not experience any anger. If I had grown up in a refugee camp, I would maybe have done the same thing that this boy did."

Her most important message is: "Do not be afraid. Fear breeds one thing only and that is hate. And hate breads violence."

In the name of truth, love and deepest healing.
Thank you and Amen.

Recommended Literature

Abouleish, Ibrahim: Sekem: A Sustainable Community in the Egyptian Desert (2005)

AnShin Thomas, Claude: At Hell's Gate: A Soldier's Journey from War to Peace (2004)

Bloch, Ernst: The Principle of Hope (1995)

Bohm, David: Wholeness and the Implicated Order (2002)

Briggs, J. u. F. D. Peat: Turbulent Mirror: An Illustrated Guide to Chaos Theory and the Science of Wholeness (1990)

Chardin, Teilhard de: The Phenomenon of Man (1976)

Coats, Callum: Living Energies: Exposition of Concepts Viktor Schauberger (2002)

Duhm, Dieter: Synthese der Wissenschaft (1979)

Duhm, Dieter: Politische Texte für eine gewaltfreie Erde (1992)

Duhm, Dieter: Towards a New Culture (As copy available. Please contact Verlag Meiga)

Duhm, Dieter: Eros Unredeemed (As copy available. Please contact Verlag Meiga)

Duhm, Dieter: The Sacred Matrix, Verlag Meiga (2006)

Frère Roger: His Love Is a Fire (1990)

Fukuoka, Masanobu: The One-Straw Revolution (1985)

Geusen, Madjana (Hrsg.): Man's Holy Grail Is Woman. Paintings, drawings and texts by Dieter Duhm (2006)

Goldsmith, Edward, Jerry Mander: The Case Against the Global Economy (2001)

Hillesum, Etty: The Letters and Diaries 1941-1943 (2002)

Holzer, Sepp: The Rebel Farmer (2004)

Kleinhammes, Sabine (Hrsg.): Rettet den Sex – Ein Manifest von Frauen für einen neuen sexuellen Humanismus (1988)

Krystal, Phyllis: Sai Baba: The Ultimate Experience (1995)

Kübler-Ross, Elisabeth: Death (1997)

Lawlor, Robert: Voices of the First Day: Awakening in the

Aboriginal Dreamtime (1991)
Leonard, George: The Silent Pulse (2006)
Lichtenfels, Sabine: GRACE. Pilgrimage for a Future without War (2007)
Lichtenfels, Sabine: Sources of Love and Peace (2004)
Lichtenfels, Sabine: Traumsteine (2000)
Lichtenfels, Sabine: Weiche Macht (1996)
Lovelock, James: The Ages of Gaia: a Biography of Our Living Earth (1995)
Lusseyran, Jacques: And There Was Light (1987)
Lusseyran, Jacques: What One Sees Without Eyes (1999)
Margulis, Lynn: Early Life (2002)
Margulis, Lynn: Symbiotic Planet: A New Look at Evolution (2000)
McLean, Dorothee: To Hear the Angels Sing: An Odyssey of Co-Creation with the Devic Kingdom (1991)
Miller, Alice: Breaking Down the Wall of Silence: To Join the Waiting Child (1997)
Miller, Alice: Am Anfang war Erziehung (1980)
Morgan, Marlo: Mutant Message Down Under. A Woman's Journey into Dreamtime Australia. (1995)
Mulford, Prentice: The Use and Necessity of Recreation (2005)
Peace Pilgrim: Her Life and Work in Her Own Words (1992)
Pogacnik, Marco: Healing the Heart of the Earth (1998)
Reich, Wilhelm: The Mass Psychology of Fascism (1975)
Satprem: On the Way to Supermanhood (1986)
Satprem: Sri Aurobindo or the Adventure of Consciousness (1993)
Schwenk, Theodor: Sensitive Chaos (1996)
Talbot, Michael: Holographic Universe (1996)
Unesco: Gloria Cuartas: Mayor of Apartad Pal (1998)
Ywahoo, Dhyani: Voices of our Ancestors (1988)
Zillmer, Hans Joachim: Darwin's Mistake: Antediluvian Discoveries Prove: Dinosaurs and Humans Co-Existed (1998)
Zorn, Fritz: Mars (1982)

Further Information:

The "Plan of the Healing Biotopes", as it is described in this book, is a complex vision based on over 25 years practiced research. An ever growing team of highly committed people are working all over the world to carry it out. What they work on are still prototypes. As with all cutting edge research these models are experiments and need time and resources for their development. Sustainable funding is urgently needed. Whoever is willing to support, please contact the Institute for Global Peacework or donate to:

IHC - International Humanities Center

POBox 923, Malibu, CA 90265, USA
Pay to: IHC/**IGF**
For credit card payments please call IHC:
+1-310-579.2069 (Fax: +1-206-333.1797)

Institute for Global Peacework
Monte Cerro
P – 7630 Colos
Portugal
Tel.: + 351 – 283 635 484
Fax.: + 351 - 283 635 374
email: igf@tamera.org
www.tamera.org

LaVergne, TN USA
23 November 2010
206072LV00003B/120/A